Faith & New Testament Fallacies

Birth of Christianity & Related Articles

By
Doyle E.
Duke

PRAISE FOR FAITH & NEW TESTAMENT FALLACIES

*F*aith and New Testament Fallacies is not for everyone; it will confound those looking for simple answers or simple-minded polemics on any side. It will not satisfy believers unwilling to have their ideas and faith intelligently questioned, or unbelievers unwilling to learn some church history and to become knowledgeable about biblical concepts as well as contradictions—and to grapple with what the Bible (especially the New Testament) really says. It challenges Christians who may not want to be challenged. It could well embarrass Christians confident that although they do not understand scripture, it is surely only because "God moves in a mysterious way His wonders to perform" (as poet William Cowper put it). Here is a thoughtful man, Doyle Duke, who does understand the Bible and can explain it to those willing to read and to think.

The book is not without its flaws; it needs a bit more coherence. It is a collection of interesting, well argued essays, but it would be improved by better editing those essays into a book-length narrative that develops themes and argues in a somewhat more organized way. The occasional repetition of points is understandable in a collection of stand-alone essays, but could be reduced with a bit more editorial care.

Dr. Ed Buckner—former Executive Director of the Council for Secular Humanism, form President of American Atheists, co-author w/ son Michael Buckner of *Freedom We Trust*.

Cover composition by Doyle E. Duke, Duke Publishing, using Photoshop techniques.

Library of Congress Cataloging-in-Publication Data

Doyle E. Duke, Union Grove, Alabama

Faith and New Testament Fallacies: Birth of Christianity and Related Articles

p.c.m. (Duke Publishing-2018). ISBN 978-1-64066-052-6 (paperback); ISBN 978-1-64066-058-8 (eBook mobi Kindle version)

Library of Congress Control Number 2018963361

Library of Congress Subject Headings

- Christianity--Criticism and interpretation.
- Christianity--Philosophy.

BISAC Subject Headings

REL006080 RELIGION / Biblical Criticism & Interpretation / General

PHI022000 PHILOSOPHY / Religious

First Edition (© 2018)

TABLE OF CONTENTS

FOREWORD

As a means of promoting this book, I solicited uncompensated reviews. Because of it's nature, I knew I would receive opposing views from both theist and non-theist. Some of those critical reviews were quite scathing, but I welcomed them. First, because they revealed the types, and in many cases, the substance of objections I had to address. Secondly, they provided a glimpse into the character and intellect of the person who would find fault with my endeavor.

Most of the objections I've received only enforce my opinions. The biggest fallacy I've noted is that they base their understanding upon the research and writings of theologians, historians, and scholars of the pre-Enlightenment point of view, who rely on the historical-critical method to study biblical narratives rather than the textual analysis of biblical sources. I base my argument upon one that went through the fire of criticism 1900 years ago. That is: if the New Testament is suppose to be harmonious, readily discernible, and surely intended to be understood by the early readers, why do we need 18th century scholars to decipher its meaning? Why hasn't someone explained the obvious contradictions, interpolations, and outright lies? Why have none of my reviewers even address my postulate? I can only assume that my poor writing skills have failed me.

My opponents content that I'm a poor writer with a limited educational background, and rightly so. I am a self-taught writer and Bible scholar. However, while I lack formal education, I believe I've one form of training that few scholars gained during years of university and theological training. Before the introduction of the Internet, and finger-tip information, I spent years with a Bible and a concordance searching for and recording every incident of word occurrences and usage for topics such as Jesus, holy spirit, law, commandments, etc., in Hebrew or Greek. I then wrote a thesis for each word in an attempt to grasp the intended use or meaning.

This method of study may seem strange for the educated, but I think I had a good teacher. My father-in-law, who was a simple man with limited formal education, had a seemingly unlimited amount of common sense. He once told me a tale of two old farmers who met on opposite banks of a creek while riding mules. As they met in mid-stream they pause to let their mounts drink and exchange greetings. They were poor and neither could afford a saddle, one used a blanket the other appeared to have an old quilt folded underneath him.

"How you trade mules," one asked, "as is, right here in the creek?"

The other fellow had been studying his neighbors mule. "Even, I reckon."

So, they switched mounts, right there, and went their way. It wasn't until the farmer got home and pulled the quilt off his new mount that he discovered the quilt had been padded and filled the mule's sway back.

You might be wonder how this ties in with Biblical study. It just seems to enforce my philosophy: if you're trading mules you don't start your study in the middle or ass-end. You start with the teeth, at the beginning. When you give careful consideration to the "teeth" of the New Testament you find false teeth, poligripped with faith.

Seems to me, if God wanted his believers to know his word he wouldn't have had it recorded in such a matter that it would take 1700 years for scholars to figure it out. Seems to me, the only reason such efforts would be necessary would be if someone screwed it up somewhere down the line. And wouldn't you know—I was right!

In regard to this book, I have even been accused of postulating nothing; and offering only the choice of believing in Christianity or believing in nothing. This same critic stated: " You cannot create a world view without accepting something being as true without proof —you have to believe, for one thing, that the ideas of true and false are meaningful! So everyone takes something on faith."

This is the crux of my postulation: "You cannot create a world view without accepting something being as true without proof ... ." Yet, Christians accept, and insist, that a human is the son of a god, that he was born of a virgin, rose from the dead, assented to heaven, is immortal, and offers eternal life—without a shred of evidence. That is accepting a lot on faith. In contrast, I am accused of questioning such assertions without proof, or acknowledging the fine minds of historical scholars who search for gems in dusty volumes of fables and Church propaganda. And *I* believe in nothing?

Here is my postulation. The *Story of Jesus*, as alluded to earlier, declares that Jesus sent his disciples into the world to teach salvation through his death and resurrection. It asserts that those disciples became the first Christians and were the progenitors of Christianity as we know it today. A very brief description, but I believe an apt one for my purpose. What Christians ignore is the fact that there is not one topic in their story, but two contradicting tales.

The first, as mentioned, is that of a resurrected Jesus Christ who brings salvation to the world. The other is of the same Jesus, but as a Jewish messiah. All through the Gospels, the Book of Acts, and much of Paul's writings these two stores twist and intertwine like barbed wire, and wherever they cross we find a sharp discrepancy.

The Jews, even today, have not accepted either version. If they acknowledge the man Jesus it is generally as a minor Jewish prophet. Contrarily, Christianity has created an entirely new religion from folklore.

The purpose of this work is an attempt to chose between the conflicting statements and events, and present a logical interpretation of an impossible story. In the following articles I've presented scriptural proofs of contradictions, interpolation, and distortions. If you'll set aside all your preconceived notions and faith-based training you should be able to discern that they do not harmonize with today's acceptable interpretation of the *Bible Story of Jesus*. That is, the universal story touted as the path to eternal salvation.

⁓

I have no formal theological training, but I've spent over thirty years as a dedicated, practicing, Christian. During those years my foremost goal was a greater understanding of "God's word," that I might better serve Him. In almost every prayer I pleaded for understanding. I suppose that, in a sense, my prayers were answered because I now see Christianity for what it is—another empty religion.

If we accept the premise that Yahweh, or Jehovah, the God of the Old Testament, is the one, true God; then Christianity is a hoax. And were the man identified as Jesus the Christ alive, and on earth today he would rent his clothes in horror at the abomination that bears his name. Why? Because he brought a message he believed was from the one true God and man ignored the message and made a god of the messenger.

The truth is easy to discern because the Church, in its self-righteousness, hasn't even tried to hide its treachery and mistakes. The proof is readily available in most good libraries, on the Internet and even in the Catholic Church's own publication, *The Catholic Encyclopedia*. The stumbling block to that truth is finding the courage to question ingrained teachings and recognize the errors.

Faith is the backbone and glue of Christianity. You have been told there is no salvation without faith. You have been told that to doubt is damnable. You have been taught that the 'spirit' will guide you. You have been led to believe that the Church is the curator of all knowledge, and you believe the Church would never practice deception. You have been deceived on all counts. Christianity uses faith as blinders to cover the gaping flaws in its doctrines. Now, if you will give me the opportunity, I will give you proof. If you will not accept fact and sound reasoning over faith then you wish to remain in ignorance and no amount of evidence will move you. But read on, you might pick up at least one bit of knowledge from this missive.

⌀⦚⌀

The first *Catholic Encyclopedia: an International Work of Reference on the Constitution, Doctrine, Discipline, and History of the Catholic Church* was compiled and published on April 19, 1913. From its inception, it was praised by both Catholics and Protestants as one of the greatest sources of Church information every presented, but it did incite criticism as well as praise. The compilers had attempted to present an honest and truthful history of their institution, with the prevailing social and historical environments as they pertained to the Church. This work covers almost every conceivable topic relative to the Catholic Church from its inception, and pulls no punches.

It contains some of the most horrendous and damning tales any organization ever admitted freely and publicly. Why? I can only surmise that it was because, at the time the deeds were condoned and committed, it was the way of the world and the Church officials believed they were acting with the best interests of the Church in mind.

In 1996, a young man named Kelvin Knight was inspired to make the Catholic Encyclopedia readily and freely available to everyone via the Internet. He launched a Web site and solicited submissions from anyone who had a copy, or access to a copy, of the 1913 edition of the encyclopedia. As submissions came in, he proofed, corrected, and added each article to the Web to create The *New Advent Catholic Encyclopedia*. Of course, you're wondering: "Why the 1913 edition?" Its copyright limitation had expired, so he was free from all liability and red tape.

In 2006, *Catholic Answers* decided to take on the monumental task of publishing an authoritative online version to prevent and correct "… (both accidental and purposeful), missing articles, and in the worse cases, changed meanings." The result was a version of the encyclopedia complete with additional explanations and justifications to clarify some of the more controversial topics. As a result, to avoid any copyright violations, my Catholic encyclopedia references in these articles refer the reader to the *Original* (or Old) *Catholic Encyclopedia* (1913 edition) that is still online. You may also use the *Catholic Answers* and do an alphabetical search to find the topic and make a quote search. I cannot stress the importance of the earlier encyclopedias as a must reference source.

Because Christians turn to the Bible as their final authority, I often find myself forced to refer to or quote passages from the New Testament Scriptures as if they were authoritative. Such instances are only to dispute a point or present an argument, not to lent validation. In addition, I have capitalized the word Apostles whenever it refers directly or indirectly to those allegedly chosen by Jesus. I have also capitalized the word scriptures when references the Christian Bible or Hebrew Scriptures.

Since this is a compilation of articles I have written, some redundancies have occurred. I've tried to limit such instances, but in order to maintain article integrity I felt it best to leave some. I apologize for any distraction this may cause.

You may also recognize familiar passages if you've read my earlier book *The Amazing Deception: A Critical Analysis of Christianity*. I have quoted freely from it.

⌐✦⌐

The first *Catholic Encyclopedia: an International Work of Reference on the Constitution, Doctrine, Discipline, and History of the Catholic Church* was compiled and published on April 19, 1913. From its inception, it was praised by both Catholics and Protestants as one of the greatest sources of Church information every presented, but it did incite criticism as well as praise. The compilers had attempted to present an honest and truthful history of their institution, with the prevailing social and historical environments as they pertained to the Church. This work covers almost every conceivable topic relative to the Catholic Church from its inception, and pulls no punches. It contains some of the most horrendous and damning tales any organization ever admitted freely and publicly. Why? I can only surmise that it was because, at the time the deeds were condoned and committed, it was the way of the world and the Church officials believed they were acting with the best interests of the Church in mind.

In 1996, a young man named Kelvin Knight was inspired to make the Catholic Encyclopedia readily and freely available to everyone via the Internet. He launched a Web site and solicited submissions from anyone who had a copy, or access to a copy, of the 1913 edition of the encyclopedia. As submissions came in, he proofed, corrected, and added each article to the Web to create The *New Advent Catholic Encyclopedia*. Of course, you're wondering: "Why the 1913 edition?" Its copyright limitation had expired, so he was free from all liability and red tape.

In 2006, *Catholic Answers* decided to take on the monumental task of publishing an authoritative online version to prevent and correct "... (both accidental and purposeful), missing articles, and in the worse cases, changed meanings." The result was a version of the encyclopedia complete with additional explanations and justifications to clarify some of the more controversial topics. As a result, to avoid any copyright violations, my Catholic encyclopedia references in these articles refer the reader to the *Original* (or Old) *Catholic Encyclopedia* (1913 edition) that is still online. You may also use the *Catholic Answers* and do an alphabetical search to find the topic and make a quote search. I cannot stress the importance of the earlier encyclopedias as a must reference source.

Because Christians turn to the Bible as their final authority, I often find myself forced to refer to or quote passages from the New Testament Scriptures as if they were authoritative. Such instances are only to dispute a point or present an argument, not to lent validation. In addition, I have capitalized the word Apostles whenever it refers directly or indirectly to those allegedly chosen by Jesus. I have also capitalized the word scripture when references the Christian Bible and law when referring to the Hebrew Law in any context—quotes excepted.

Since this is a compilation of articles I have written, some redundancies have occurred. I've tried to limit such instances, but in order to maintain article integrity I felt it best to leave some. I apologize for any distraction this may cause.

You may also recognize familiar passages if you've read my earlier book *The Amazing Deception: A Critical Analysis of Christianity.* I have quoted freely from it.

BIRTH OF CHRISTIANITY

Birth of Christianity is a brief but intense history of
Christianity that reveals some little known or seldom
mentioned facts that should give the reader pause for thought.

When I was a Christian, I turned to the Bible, especially the
New Testament, to solve every problem I confronted. I
often found the answers in the epistles of Peter, James,
or John; and I learned of Jesus the Christ within the Gospels. It was
reassuring to be able to read the very words of those who knew and
walked with my Lord. For years, I believed the New Testament was a
canonization of letters written by the followers of Jesus to the various
churches in Asia Minor, Greece, and Rome. Imagine my shock when
I learned Matthew, Mark, and John did not write the Gospels, and
little is known of Luke! Imagine the further shock when I discovered
that Paul was the earliest writer and the only one whose writings can
be proven with any degree of credibility. Yes, it's true. Upon further
study, I found that such is common knowledge among theologians
and historians, and is a general subject in most theological
seminaries. I also discovered that the selection and canonization of
the New Testament books was anything but the holy and dignified
process I had assumed it to be. I believed that righteous, impartial,
and charismatic men of God came together, perhaps prayerfully,
to choose the holy writings for God's New Testament. Instead, I
discovered tales of angry, power-hungry, vicious men leading mobs
of incited thugs, sailors, and dock-workers into armed combat to
enforce their will. I read of ghetto type gangs clashing in the streets
and meeting halls. I read of venomous speeches and hateful slurs
screamed back and forth, and in one incident—murder—committed
in a fit of rage.

It is with total assurance that Christians base their religion on what they believe is the uncorrupted, if not inerrant, word of their God—the Bible. There are those who claim the Bible, as the inspired Word of God, is infallible and completely error free. Others allow for human errors in the copying and translation of that work, and might even admit to minor inconsistencies. Still, they will insist that in no way has the intent been corrupted. Some claim the book possesses a timeless, magical quality that gives it the ability to conform to the various social and civil conditions that have evolved through the ages. Others concede that some changes in interpretation have been necessary—most notably, the difference in the literal observance of the Hebraic Law and the spiritual interpretation introduced by Christians.

Although the Christian religion is fraught with thousands of differing denominations and an endless number of personal interpretations there are a few mutually accepted doctrines that, for the most part, are held as indisputable. Some of the foremost are that Jesus Christ is the son of God, that he was crucified for the believer's sins and arose on the third day, and that the Bible is the divine word of God. All this, of course, must be accepted by faith. The necessity of such a faith-based belief becomes obvious when one realizes there is absolutely no logical or conclusive evidence available to prove the astounding claims made by adherents.

Today, in the United States and most Christian nations, there is much attention and contention given to the differences between liberal and conservative Christianity. Here I am tempted to make the statement that this contention is bringing the credibility of Christianity into question and causing a decline in church attendance. However, that statement would not be true. The real reason for the decline in attendance is the increase in available knowledge (think Internet) and the individual's ability to discern truth. Religions thrive among the ignorant—those who lack knowledge, or those who embrace faith and refuse to question the source or validity of their beliefs. Today, more and more people, especially young people, are able to look beyond the fables and superstitions that have deceived believers for centuries, and make choices based upon reason, logic, and scientific facts. The result has created a widening gulf between those Christians who believe in a literal interpretation of the Bible, and those who are willing to accept allegorical interpretations. At one end of the spectrum are those ultra-conservatives who cling stubbornly to their faith and believe that every word in the Bible is the literal, infallible word of God. Contrarily, you will find the ultra-liberals who want to believe in God, but are willing to embrace compromises. Between these extremes are thousands of differing denominations, and yet, despite all the division, almost all agree upon the history of their shared religion. However, few realize that much of that history—even the origin of their religion—has been fabricated.

⸎

The origin of Christianity does not begin with the man Jesus—or Paul of Tarsus. The idea of Christianity began with the clash of Judaism and Grecian Hellenism. Alexander the Great's most earth-shaking feat was not the conquest of Asia Minor. His greatest contribution to history was the introduction of Grecian thought and philosophy into the ignorant and backward cultures of those nations he subdued. Many of the people he conquered came to revere him as a deliverer, and in some cases, they even deified him as a god or super-hero. Judea and the Jews were no exception. They were drawn to the richness and opulence of the Hellenist lifestyle. A comparison might be made to a country-boy's first visit to the city. Only in this case, the city was delivered to the boy. The austere Jewish lifestyle could not compete with the gaiety of the games, circuses, and lascivious customs of the Greeks. But even more attractive were Grecian knowledge and the freedom from ignorance it offered. Grecian Hellenism flourished long after the death of Alexander and the division of his empire. Where, at first, the Jewish elders bewailed the seduction of their youth, they later decried the corruption of their rulers as they adopted Hellenist values and Grecian names.

Much of that Hellenistic knowledge was introduced in the form of Grecian philosophy. The Jews could not resist the discoveries and teachings of such great minds as Socrates, Plato, Thales, and Aristotle. But the collision of cultures necessitated an exchange of values. While the Jews were drawn to the knowledge of the Greeks, the Western world was attracted by the Jews' concept of a monotheistic god.

From the time of Pythagoras (584 BCE), the search for knowledge obsessed the Greeks. Every aspect of life was relegated to a philosophy or science: metaphysics, epistemology, aesthetics, politics, logic, languages, and religion. Today, it is hard to imagine the fervor that was associated with the search for new knowledge. It was taught in schools, discussed in meetings, and argued in the streets. The whole world was a classroom where new ideas were welcomed, discussed, and dissected. Man's understanding of life and the world about him was opening new vistas of knowledge, and with that knowledge came the freedom from the fear and ignorance of superstition. But understand, this knowledge was not complete. For while men might be able to predict the movement of the stars, relate music to mathematical principals, trace the origin of plants and animals, measure the earth, or identify the atom religion was still very much a mystery because it could not be measured or proven. Despite the advanced knowledge, most people were still confounded by the assertions of numerous priests professing a panoply of gods and goddesses. Is it any wonder then that the simple idea of one supreme god was attractive?

Even so, while the idea might be attractive, some aspects of Jewish worship were simply unacceptable for inquiring minds. Foremost among those objectionable ideas were those of circumcision, the separation of races, physical contamination, and a god who rejected all Gentiles, which, of course, excluded them. And while they were willing to accept some of the miraculous Biblical stories, some stretched their sensibilities. The results were attempts to develop speculative and philosophical justification for Judaism in terms of Greek philosophy.

One of the earliest to try, though by no means the first, was Philo of Alexandria. While many Grecian and Hellenistic Jewish philosophers were endeavoring to forge a union between the two cultures, Philo was one of the first whose writings have survived. He was a Hellenized Jew whose life spanned the introduction to the new millennium, from about 20 BCE to 50 CE. He was contemporaneous with Jesus but there is no reason to believe they ever met. Philo produced a combination of both traditions that developed concepts for future Hellenistic interpretation of messianic Hebrew thought. His concepts were used by Clements of Alexandria and other Christian Apologists, such as Athenagoras, Theophilus, Justin Martyr, Tertullian, and Origin. In addition, it is almost certain that he influenced Paul and the authors of the Gospel of John and the

Epistle to the Hebrews. In the process, he laid the foundation for the development of Christianity as we know it today. Although Philo was thoroughly educated in Greek philosophy and culture and had a deep regard for Plato, Aristotelian logic, and Pythagorean ideas, he regarded the Jewish teachings of Moses as "the summit of philosophy." He considered Moses the teacher of Pythagoras and of all Greek philosophers. For him, as with many philosophers of the first and second century, Greek philosophy was a natural development of the revelatory teachings of Moses. Before Jesus, or Paul, were ever born a search for *Christianity* (a union between Judaism and Hellenism) was already underway.

Philo's most developed doctrine, on which all his philosophical system hung, was that of the Logos. By developing this doctrine he fused Greek philosophical concepts with Hebrew religious thought and provided the foundation for Christianity by presenting the idea of a mediator—the Logos—between man and God. The same concept used in John's speculations, and later, in the Hellenistic Christian Logos and the Gnostic doctrines of the second century. In essences, what we have is the philosophy that enabled Paul to develop his concept of Jesus as the Logos, or the Christ.

⊷◦✿◦⊶

The idea that Jesus developed, or introduced, the doctrine of a redeeming savior just isn't possible. Jesus was most likely either a Pharisee—despite his condemnations, not all Pharisees were wicked—or a member of the Essences, who was sent to announce the coming kingdom, and was crucified because he proclaimed himself a king—the king of the Jews. What he did teach was a simple, clear message that is stated repeatedly throughout the Synoptic Gospels: the Kingdom of God. *The Kingdom of God is nigh ... they shall sit down in the Kingdom of God ... the kingdom of God is preached, and every man presseth into it ... the kingdom of God cometh not with observation ... the kingdom of God is within you.* What did all these sayings mean? The Messiah was coming to usher in the Kingdom of God promised in Zechariah 9:9&10.

> Rejoice greatly, O daughter of Zion; shout, O daughter of Jerusalem: behold, thy King cometh unto thee: he is just, and

having salvation; lowly, and riding upon an ass, and upon a colt the foal of an ass.

And I will cut off the chariot from Ephraim, and the horse from Jerusalem, and the battle bow shall be cut off: and he shall speak peace unto the heathen: and his dominion shall be from sea even to sea, and from the river even to the ends of the earth.

That Jesus believed this to be his mission is made evident by his entrance into Jerusalem on Palm Sunday, which he engineered in an effort to fulfill this prophesy. That he was crucified as a rebel who presented himself as the king of the Jews is make obvious by the inscription on his cross that mockingly proclaimed him as such.

Before I proceed further, I'd like to address a premise held by most Christians, that some Scriptures such as these just quoted have a literal, and prophetic meaning that fore-tells the coming of Jesus as the Christ. There are a number of factors that deny such an assertion: If such were the case, any reference would indicate the Jewish messiah, not a gentile Christ because the Jews had never heard of such a concept until the advent of Paul. Scriptures used to make such claims are taken out of context, omit obvious contradictions from the original Scriptures, and are often taken from two, three, or even four separate sections of the Hebrew Bible to form a false statement.

Some Jews looked for a warrior Messiah in the character of David, others believed that their Messiah would gather a following and march upon the temple. When that happened, God and his holy army would swoop down and destroy the Romans, and institute worldwide peace. Then God would assume his throne in Jerusalem. However, proclaiming one's self king of the Jews and attacking the money-changers was considered open rebellion against Rome. The standard penalty was crucifixion.

Jesus was a Jew and as such obeyed the Mosaic Law, which conflicted with Hellenistic philosophies. In addition, though Christians claim he taught salvation through a belief in his resurrection, the values he taught his Apostles deny such an assertion. In fact, the Catholic Encyclopedia refers to the members of the Jerusalem church as "judazing Christians," when in fact they never wavered from their faith.

Throughout the Gospels, we find Jesus preaching salvation through his person or sending his disciples to spread the gospel to all the world. Almost simultaneously, there are incidents where he is teaching the Law and damning those who would corrupt even the smallest article. In the New Testament and secular works there are records of the Apostles teaching Christianity throughout the known world, despite incidents where they are obviously observing the Law. However, a close study of the Apostles reveals they knew nothing of a commission to the Gentiles prior to Paul, and taught salvation through the Law. They are defending the Law when Paul is called to Jerusalem to discuss circumcision (Acts 15 & Gal. 2:7-9). Peter was observing the Law when Cornelius sent for him (Acts 10:28).The Jerusalem Church was observing the Law and attempting to validate Paul's sincerity when he was taken in the temple (Acts 21:21).

In the year 58 A.D., approximately twenty-five years after the crucifixion; the Jews, including James, were still observing the Law—as they were taught by their master. Paul was not a popular man among the Jews and many thought of him as one who would destroy the Law. In an attempt to get him to take a vow one of the leaders, probably James, the brother of Jesus, said to him, "Thou seest brother, how many thousands of Jews there are which believe; and they are all zealous of the law." [Jews who believe ... believe what? The subject was obviously not the Law, that was a given. They believed in Jesus; but as the Messiah. The Apostles were Jews, they were in the temple, and they kept the Law.]

Since one belief is incompatible with the other, and since Jesus' Apostles were still observing the Law and contending with Paul concerning it after Jesus' death, we must assume they did not view Jesus as Paul's Christ. The incident in Acts 2:14, where Peter stood with the eleven and preached Jesus Christ might come to mind. If any such events did occur, then Peter had to be referring to the Jewish Messiah, not the Christian Christ, because the setting and audience were Jewish. In addition, Paul claimed credit for introducing Jesus the Christ and Paul had not yet been converted. Peter's statement in Acts 15:7-11 is an obvious interpolation because it has him describing the Law as a burden, or yoke, (verse 10) that neither they nor their fathers were able to bear—yet he continued to teach and keep it. Peter is even made to say: "...we believe that through the grace of the

Lord Jesus Christ we shall be saved, even as they." This begs answers to a few questions: (1) Why were the Apostles still observing the Law instead of switching to Paul's alternative plan? (2) Why were they in disagreement over the issue of circumcision? (3) Why were the Apostles trying to get Paul's confirmation of the Law years later when he was set upon in the temple prior to his arrest? And (4) why didn't the Apostles come to Paul's defense?

When you understand that the inclusion of Gentiles originated with Paul, not Jesus, other questions arise. Why did Jesus hand pick his disciples—allegedly, even requiring that the replacement for Judas be one who had known him, Jesus, personally—then reveal a different and contrary set of teachings to Paul; and that only by a vision no one else could collaborate? Gentiles were already accepted under Old Testament Law, but only as circumcised Jews. We have only Paul's word that they were not under the Law.

And in Hebrews we find a passage that negates Paul's authority:

> And for this cause he is the mediator of the new testament, that by means of death, for the redemption of the transgressions that were under the first testament, they which are called might receive the promise of eternal inheritance. For where a testament is, there must also of necessity be the death of the testator. For a testament is of force after men are dead: otherwise it is of no strength at all while the testator liveth. In the case of a will, it is necessary to prove the death of the one who made it because a will is in force only when somebody has died; it never takes effect while the one who made it is living. (Heb 9:15-17)

It never takes effect while the one who made it is living. Neither can it be changed after that one is dead! If Jesus was the mediator of a new covenant then that covenant would have been in effect at his death and could not have been changed to accommodate Paul's teachings.

And referring to the Abrahamic covenant Paul negates his own argument:

> Brethren, I speak after the manner of men; Though it be but a man's covenant, yet if it be confirmed, no man disannulleth, or addeth thereto. (Gal 3:15)

With these scriptures in mind I ask, why didn't Jesus reveal Paul's teachings to the disciples? How could it be part of the New Testament covenant if it was introduced after the "reading of the will"? An act forbidden according to Gal 3:15.

> I am the Lord: that is my name: and my glory will I not give to another, neither my praise to graven images. Behold, the former things are come to pass, and new things do I declare before they spring forth I tell you of them. (Is. 42:8 & 9)

Study of the Old Testament reveals these two facts; God is supreme and jealous, not sharing his glory with any. And he was always specific and clear about his laws and commandments, even dictating numerous books concerning their observance. His people might backslide and err, even forget his will, but never because he sprang a surprise covenant upon them.

I'm aware that Christians teach that the Law was "fulfilled in Christ." But if that were so, why did Jesus send his Apostles to preach the Law to the "... lost sheep of the house of Israel" (Matt. 10:6, 15:24)? Why were they contending with Paul about the Law and why did they continue to observe it? Why were they and thousands of Jewish believers keeping it (Acts 10:14, 15, 21:10)? Why did Paul profess to believe the Law (Acts 24:14) when he was attempting to destroy it? And why did Jesus say it would not change until heaven and earth passed away?

A careful and objective reading of Paul's works reveal that he was not only voiding jots and tittles, but blatantly contradicting almost every commandment in the Law. Why? Because the Jewish Law was what differentiated between a Jew and a Gentile—or a Hellenistic Jew—and Paul was determined to shatter that barrier. But what of Jesus' Apostles? Didn't Jesus send them to preach Christianity to all nations? No! He did not. This corruption is one of many interpolations that can be found throughout the Gospels and Acts. One such incident is found in Luke 24, and Matt. 28:19 where a risen Jesus commissioned his Apostles to "Go ye therefore, and teach all nations, baptizing them in the name of the Father, and of the Son, and of the Holy Ghost." This is a direct contradiction of Matt. 10:5 where Jesus commanded his Apostles to "Go not into the way of the

Gentiles, and into any city of the Samaritans enter ye not." Yes, again I know Christianity teaches the Apostles were to preach the coming Kingdom of God and that Jesus' resurrection supposedly established that kingdom, thus canceling the first commission, to the Jews.

This teaching is unsound for a number of reasons we have already mentioned; in addition, this presupposes the recognition of the trinity of the godhead, which wasn't a contention until late in the second century. From the Stanford Encyclopedia of Philosophy; section 3.1.1 *The One God in the Trinity:*

> Early Christianity was theologically diverse, although as time went on a "catholic" movement, a bishop-led, developing organization which, at least from the late second century, claimed to be the true successors of Jesus' apostles, became increasingly dominant, out-competing many gnostic and quasi-Jewish groups. Still, confining our attention to what scholars now call this "catholic" or "proto-orthodox" Christianity, it contained divergent views about the Father, Son, and Holy Spirit. No theologian in the first three Christian centuries was a trinitarian in the sense of a believing that the one God is tripersonal, containing equally divine "persons", Father, Son, and Holy Spirit.

> The terms we translate as "Trinity" (Latin: trinitas, Greek: trias) seem to have come into use only in the last two decades of the second century; but such usage doesn't reflect trinitarian belief. These late second and third century authors use such terms not to refer to the one God, but rather to refer to the plurality of the one God, together with his Son (or Word) and his Spirit. They profess a "trinity", triad or threesome, but not a triune or tripersonal God.

This gives strong evidence that these, and other conflicting passages in the Gospels, are interpolations written about the same time the Catholic Church found such writings useful. Here were little known writings, suddenly discovered when Christians, Gnostics, and Jews were contending for *authoritative* writings. And since the history of Catholicism makes it obvious there was no action too despicable for them to initiate if they believed it would further their agenda, there is no reason to doubt they would use forgery.

Further, in Matt. 10:17, 19:16, and Luke 18:18, when men asked Jesus how they might obtain eternal life did Jesus say, "Wait around a few days. I'm going to be crucified for everyone's sins, but I'll rise from the dead to be the Son of God then my disciples here will tell you what you need to do."? No. He told them to keep the Law.

Luke 24:36-53 gives a very descriptive picture of alleged events preceding the commission. The Apostles and disciples were gathered in Jerusalem for a meal when suddenly, Jesus was with them. He showed them the scars in his hands and feet and asked them to touch him. He shared their meal, gave them the commission, and told them to wait for the Holy Spirit. He opened their understanding about all things in the Law and Prophets concerning him. Then they watched him rise up into heaven.

Now, imagine you're one of those disciples, you have just seen the resurrected son of God, touched him, talked with him, shared a meal, heard his instructions to preach his message to all the world. He's revealed all the mysteries of the Law and Prophets concerning him. You've watched him levitate into the sky. A few days later, you're empowered by the Holy Spirit. Now tell me, how much of this experience would you forget? Would you forget that the Law was fulfilled in Christ and that you were to preach salvation through his death to everyone? Let's assume it is possible that one Apostle did eschew the miracles of that marvelous meeting; hard to believe, but grant it. However, according to the New Testament it wasn't just one that doubted, wavered, and turned back to the Law. All the Apostles are depicted keeping the Law throughout the Gospels and Acts!

Here is another point to ponder. In Gal. 1:11&12, Paul declares:

> But I certify you, brethren, that the gospel which was preached of me is not after man.

> For I neither received it of man, neither was I taught it, but by the revelation of Jesus Christ.

What does this mean? The Apostles did not receive a commission from Jesus that negated the Law, otherwise, they would not have continued to observe it after the alleged new commission. But Paul's instructions were different. If we would believe him, Jesus was having him destroy the Law. These two teachings are not compatible.

The Apostles, the Jerusalem Church, were not Christians; they were Messianic Jews awaiting the return of Jesus—their expected Messiah—who would lead the army of God to establish God's kingdom (Acts 4:32-5:14).

If one believes the New Testament then there can be no doubt that Jesus' Apostles kept the Law which forbade them to even associate with Gentiles. What is the significance of this? First, they were never converted to Christianity. Secondly, if Peter was never a Christian, he was not the first Catholic pope. Consequently, Christianity is a fraud.

I must admit, this was a revelation to me. I've studied the New Testament for decades and never realized the significance of these scriptures, nor have I read or heard anyone else offer such a conjecture. I'm I the first to come to this conclusion? No. I'm not so naive or vain to think others haven't discovered this truth. So why haven't they introduced it into the Church—or the world? That it wasn't announced during the first fifteen hundred years of Catholicism is understandable; only the clergy could read or interpret scripture. Anyone suggesting any idea so radical would have been burned as a heretic.

With the emergence of Protestantism and the Enlightenment, Biblical interpretation passed to the individual. Why, then, didn't this subject become a topic for discussion? I believe it did. I've no doubt that many theologians and lay-members have struggled with this contradiction and chose to believe the interpolations because the truth is too damning to contemplate.

Still, there is the possibility that the Apostles converted after the chronological ending of the New Testament, but with Paul, their nemesis removed, and the advent of the Jewish Wars coming so soon afterward, I don't believe there would have been enough incentive nor time to erode the beliefs of all the Apostles.

The earliest followers of Jesus were called Nazarenes and later, the Ebionites.

The Ebionite/Nazarene movement was made up of mostly Jewish/ Israelite followers of John the Baptizer and later Jesus, who were concentrated in Palestine and surrounding regions and led by "James the Just" (the oldest brother of Jesus), and flourished between the years 30-80 C.E. They were zealous for the Torah

and continued to walk in all the mitzvot (commandments) as enlightened by their Rabbi and Teacher, but accepted non-Jews into their fellowship on the basis of some version of the Noachide Laws (Acts 15 and 21). The term Ebionite (from Hebrew 'Evyonim) means "Poor Ones" and was taken from the teachings of Jesus: "Blessed are you Poor Ones, for yours is the Kingdom of God" based on Isaiah 66:2 and other related texts that address a remnant group of faithful ones. Nazarene comes from the Hebrew word Netzer (drawn from Isaiah 11:1) and means "a Branch"—so the Nazarenes were the "Branchites" or followers of the one they believed to be the Branch. The term Nazarene was likely the one first used for these followers of Jesus, as evidenced by Acts 24:5 where Paul is called "the ringleader of the sect of the Nazarenes."
The Jewish Roman World of Jesus - Dr. James Tabor

I believe the greatest confusion concerning the role of Jesus comes from the use of the words *Christ* and *Messiah*. When we read the word Christ in our English New Testament, we must remember that if the original manuscripts were Jewish then they would have been written in Hebrew and the translation would be Messiah—the Jews' expected deliverer. However, the writers, or translators, of the New Testament Gospels were Gentiles or Hellenistic Jews—Jews of the Diaspora. Those Hellenistic Jews had accepted Grecian ways to the point where they had lost their ability to speak Aramaic and, in many cases, read Hebrew. Centuries earlier, to facilitate the study of the Law, they had translated the Old Testament into the Greek language. That translation was called the Septuagint. When the word messiah was transposed to the Greek word Christ, it led to a corruption in meaning because the Greeks had a concept of a son of god where the Jews did not. Therefore we should consider the context and setting in which the word is used in deciding whether the speaker is referring to Jesus the Christ, Jesus the Messiah, or if it is part of an interpolation.

In actuality, Christianity is a combination of Judaism, Essene doctrines, Hellenistic philosophy, the mystery religions, and Paul's own interpretations of all four. Paul was the apostle to the Gentiles because he was the one who concocted a philosophy, and ministry, that circumvented the exclusion of Gentiles, and thereby allowed them access to the Hebrew God. For this reason, there can be no doubt that Paul was the originator of the religion known as Christianity—but not as we know it today. Other sects and philosophers were teaching hybrid forms of Hebrew Law/Hellenistic philosophy and some termed themselves Christians, but none provided Gentiles a spiritual union with the Hebrew God or taught a resurrected savior. Paul is also identified as the originator because many Christian teachings originated within his writings. It was Paul who contended with the Apostles of Jesus on such matters as circumcision, association with Gentiles, the efficacy of the Law, food offered to idols, and the indwelling of the Holy Spirit. And, though he was the one who introduced the concept of salvation through Jesus Christ, a careful reading of his writings and the Book of Acts raises question as to whether he ever mentioned that doctrine to the Apostles in Jerusalem. Paul taught Jesus Christ to the Gentiles and Hellenistic Jews outside Judea. But when he spoke to the Apostles, or before the Jerusalem Council, he became a Jew and any reference he made to Jesus or Christ may be inferred to mean the Messiah.

> And unto the Jews I became as a Jew, that I might gain the Jews; to them that are under the law, as under the law, that I might gain them that are under the law;
>
> To them that are without law, as without law, (being not without law to God, **but under the law to Christ,**) that I might gain them that are without law. (I Cor. 9:20-21) **(Emphasis added)**

The story of Paul's bold preaching of Jesus as the son of God in the synagogue, and his escape from the Jews who wanted to kill him directly after his conversion, may come to mind, (Acts chapter 9) but note that he was in Damascus, in Syria, not Judea. The fact that the Jews wanted to kill him only strengthens the theory that Paul was teaching his son of God doctrine. When he arrived in Jerusalem, the Apostles there knew him as a persecutor, and were afraid. Later, after they met, when he began speaking he must have toned his rhetoric down. The members of the *Jerusalem Church*—messianic Jews, not Christians—were told that he "preached boldly at Damascus in the name of Jesus." And later, when he preached in Jerusalem (v. 29), he again spoke boldly in the name of the Lord Jesus—no doubt avoiding the son of God, or Christ, theme.

At the Jerusalem Council (Acts 15), notice the works Paul declared: "...all the things that God had done with them." (verse 4); he and Barnabas declared, "... what miracles and wonders God had wrought among the Gentiles by them" (verse 12). There is no mention of Jesus the Christ—the son of God. Notice also, that James' decree placed only Noachian restrictions upon the gentile believers and referred them to the synagogues where they might learn the Law of Moses. James' decree indicates that they were still not Jews—still unclean and unfit for association with Jews.

The obvious picture here is one of caution, perhaps even disdain, by the Jews. Paul was a known persecutor who was teaching the Gentiles, and most likely the Jews, a doctrine contrary to the Law—a doctrine that was even exciting Jews outside Judea to physical violence. Why in the world would the Apostles be inclined to form a joint fellowship with him? To save the Gentiles? They hated the Gentiles, and were awaiting the return of Jesus to usher in the Kingdom of God and destroy them! Look at the facts: The Apostles were observing the Law. James had just decreed that they should not force the Gentiles to be circumcised. He might have even considered a *believing* Gentile would be preferable to a non-believer. His message was clear, do what you want with the Gentiles, but leave the Jews alone. When the Jerusalem church sent Judas and Silas with Paul's party (Acts 15:22-23)—that wasn't a joint missionary journey. It was a means to inform Jews along the way of what had taken place at the council, that the Gentiles were not Jews and therefore, still under the old Noachian law, still unclean.

Paul was unable to establish any churches in Judea—obviously, because the Jews rejected his concept of Jesus so adamantly they were willing to kill him. On Paul's third and last recorded visit to Jerusalem, (Acts 21) he, "...declared particularly what things God had wrought among the Gentiles by his ministry..." Did he mention Jesus the son of God? I don't think so because they, the Church elders, begin saying there were reports that he, Paul, was teaching the Jews to forsake Moses' Law, to not circumcise their children, and to not walk after the customs—all truthful accusations because Paul went first to the synagogues wherever he journeyed. The very fact that he was associating with Gentiles made him a law-breaker. They (probably James) begged him to reaffirm his observance of the Law by taking a vow. What do you think the Apostles and other Jews would have done if he'd told them that the Law was only a training aid to Jesus Christ and offered no salvation?

Paul never mentioned Jesus Christ when he was speaking to the mob after his arrest. Instead, the *person* in his vision was "Jesus of Nazareth" or "the Just One" (The Oblias, a Jewish leader). How do you suppose the crowd would have reacted if he'd preached Jesus Christ to them in the same manner he did to the Gentiles?

On the following day, when they brought Paul before the council, he again failed to tell them of Jesus the son of God. Instead, he purposely created a rift between the Pharisee and Sadducee council members by professing to be a Pharisee.

After he was turned over to Felix, the governor, Paul again faced the council in Caesarea. His defense to the charges brought against him was a simple—they can't prove anything. Then he began to lie: "But this I confess unto thee, that after the way which they call heresy, so worship I the God of my fathers, believing all things which are written in the Law and in the prophets." Paul might have believed all things, but he did not worship as his fathers. In fact, his teachings contradicted the Law. Again, there was no mention of salvation through Jesus the Christ. Later, in privacy, Paul spoke to Felix "concerning the faith in Christ," but we don't know which concept of Christ he presented.

When Paul appeared before Felix, King Agrippa, and his sister Bernice, he presented his story in a suitable manner. First he professed his innocence; then claimed he stood in hope of the promise made to the twelve tribes; that is, the blessings of Abraham, which he interpreted as meaning a resurrected Jesus—again, a Jesus of Nazareth, not Jesus the Christ. And when he tells of his conversion and vision it is Jesus who appears to him, not the son of God. Later, in Acts 26:22-23, Paul does make reference to a prophecy of *Christ* made by Moses; that he, Christ, should suffer, be the first resurrected, and be a light unto the Gentiles. Here, as was his habit, Paul mixes a couple of prophecies together to support his statement. The first is Deut. 18:15 where God, through Moses, promised the Israelites he would send them a prophet when they were settled in their land. [In the first century CE, they certainly were not settled in their land. In fact, they were on the cusp of near total annihilation.] The verses following reveal that God was promising a number of prophets. He even tells how they might identify *them*—that *they* would speak his word. Meaning, they would speak according to the Law. Paul was doing just the opposite.

The second of Paul's references is to Is. 49:6 where God promises to send *Israel* to all the earth. This is a reference to the spreading of the Law throughout the world—Israel was to carry the Mosaic Law to the Gentiles—not Paul's Jesus, and not Paul's concept of the Law. By combining Scriptures from different places in the Old Testament, Paul repeatedly took them out of context to prove what he wanted to say, and not necessarily deceitfully. It was a common practice known as *gezerah shawah*, meaning similar category. This method allowed that when similar or identical words occurred in different parts of the Law, no matter how different the context, they were identical in application. This was a common practice, used repeatedly by New Testament writers—thus, *another* reason for a corrupted New Testament. Time and time again, Paul used such techniques to give credence to his statements. And though he repeatedly denied his intent to destroy the Law, careful study will reveal that is exact what he was doing.

[For further study see my book, *The Amazing Deception: A Critical Analysis of Christianity* where I use NT Scriptures to show how Paul not only used corrupted scriptures to destroy the Law, but even became so confident as to speak for his spiritual Jesus.]

The only scriptural evidence to indicate Paul may have revealed his doctrines to the Apostles is found in Galatians where he rebuked Peter, who withdrew from the Gentiles when others from James arrived. Does this indicate Peter might not have wanted those in Jerusalem to know he'd converted to Paul's teachings, or that he'd merely erred in judgment? Perhaps he was only vacillating. Did he convert? Was he an exception? Paul's statement, in this same passage, that Peter was to go to those of the circumcision negates such questions.

Before we continue, it should be noted that with the exceptions mentioned above, nowhere else in Paul's recognized writings does he speak of a confrontation with the Apostles. And despite the fact Luke was supposed to be Paul's companion he doesn't mention Luke. In fact, Luke is only referenced twice, once in Colossians and then in II Timothy—neither are Pauline works. This is important because it is only through Luke's writings in Acts that we find personal insight into Paul and the stories of his missionary journeys. It is also important because of the numerous conflicts present in Acts.

⌐✽⌐

It should be understood that while Paul wrote letters to the churches he had established, there are no authentic writings of any of Jesus' Jewish followers. Almost without exception, all the New Testament writings are by Hellenistic Christians or gentile sympathizers. They were written late in the first century or the early second century, from forty to perhaps eighty-five years after Jesus' death, and close to two hundred years before the New Testament was canonized, toward the end of the fourth century.

Why do we have the works of Paul and none from the Apostles, even though the Apostles, as reported by Hippolytus and Eusebius, were spreading the gospel to different places? We can only guess, but there are a number of obvious factors: First, the teachings of Jesus were apocalyptic—the expectations of an eminent coming Kingdom of God. Therefore, the Apostles would have seen no need to record history or instructions for future generations—and obviously Jesus didn't teach them to do so. Jesus didn't even establish a church hierarchy or institute policies for its continuation. Secondly, if they had made records, they would have probably been destroyed in the devastations of the Jewish Wars. Thirdly, Paul's agenda was different from that of the Apostles. He obviously believed his mission to the Gentiles would require time, otherwise, why would he have worked to establish churches? Also, to encourage, instruct, and develop those churches required that he write letters. Jesus' followers, the Nazarenes, were a local group awaiting the parousia (Acts 4:34-35)—to whom would they have written?

Paul is recognized as the author of seven books: Romans, 1-2 Corinthians, Galatians, Philippians, 1 Thessalonians, and Philemon. Six other books are credited to him, but their authorship is disputed: Ephesians, Colossians, 2 Thessalonians; 1-2 Timothy, and Titus. Many reject these latter books because in them Paul is being deradicalized, sanitized, and Romanized. His stance on slavery, justification by faith, awaiting the return, and women's role has changed.

In 57 CE, Paul's second and final missionary journey ended with his arrest in Jerusalem. Philemon, was written in that same year. Christianity—allegedly first named in Antioch—was a reality. None of the other books of the New Testament were written: no Hebrews, James, or Johns. No Gospels or Acts of the Apostles. Nothing else.

Now, based solely on these seven books of Paul, what can we determine about the man Jesus? What can we state as factual? He was of the Davidic line, born of a woman, crucified and raised the son of God.

Paul never refers to any event or incident in Jesus' life. The virgin birth isn't mentioned: there's no manger, no wise men, no angels and no heavenly choir. There's no mention of his baptism or association with John and no voice from heaven or flying doves. Paul makes no reference to Jesus' ministry or miracles: no healing the sick or raising the dead, no changing of water to wine or calming the seas. Even though he repeatedly testifies of Jesus' supreme sacrifice of dying and being resurrected, Paul never mentions the details surrounding those events. There's no reference to Jesus' trial, the cross, Golgotha, earthquakes or risen saints. Why? Why is there no mention of these miraculous events? Because the Gospels and Acts were not written. If they existed, they did so as myths in the stories of ignorant men. Most likely, Paul didn't mention them because they never happened.

⊶C❋Ɔ⊷

All of the Gospels were written between 66 CE and 110 CE, but were unknown until about 130 CE, when Papias mentions Matthew and Mark. However, even this reference is ambiguous and confusing because the Matthew he refers to was written in Hebrew. The Matthew familiar to Christendom was written in Greek. It was an era of oral tradition, not writings, so Mark's writing languished for years, unnoticed, perhaps in the hands of some small Christian sect. Neither does Papias' account concerning Mark do much to commend that writer. He says Mark was the interpreter and companion of Peter in his travels. He states that Mark recorded Peter's memories of the acts and sayings of Jesus. Therefore, he never knew Jesus and supposedly wrote his gospel shortly after Peter's death, around 64 CE. The difficulties with Papias' testimony are that Peter has no significance in Mark's book and that his theology is Hellenized, like Paul's.

Papias himself seemed to care more for hearsay than for the written word. His works only survive because Eusebius quoted from Papias' *Expositions of the Sayings of the Lord*—a collection of things Papias heard said by students of the elders who claimed to have known the first disciples; in other words, oft-repeated hearsay.

> Irenaeus and Eusebius, who had the work of Papias before them, understand the Presbyters to be not Apostles, but disciples of disciples of the Lord, or even disciples of disciples of Apostles https://www.ecatholic2000.com/cathopedia/vol11/voleleven489. shtml.

Eusebius also described Papias as, "... a man of very small mind, if we may judge by his own words." In his defense, Papias offers this statement: "I did not think that information from books would help me so much as the utterances of a living and surviving voice." Here we're introduced to another historical truth, the early Christians' preference for oral rather than written tradition. It was only in the late second century that this preference began to change. Other quotations of Papias' work show how destructive this "preference for oral tradition" could be. He recorded the most bizarre claims as if they were true, such as a description of Judas' head bloated to greater than the width of a wagon trail, with his eyes lost in the flesh, and that the place where he died maintained a stench so bad that over a hundred years later, no one would go near it.

Most Christians assume that the New Testament books were written by the Apostles, or disciples for whom they are titled, or the author identified in the introduction. Nothing could be further from the truth. The original works perished in the very infancy of the Church. No Christian writer has ever made a reference to any of them. At best, what we have are edited copies of the original authors' works, or someone's reminiscence; and in some cases, highly imaginative creations credited to one of the Apostles. Most Christians, however, refuse to accept such discrepancies, believing instead that the entire Bible is the divinely inspired, inerrant, word of God—even though it is universally accepted among many historians, theologians, and paleographers that the Scriptures have been altered.

There are thousands of books, in public libraries, in bookstores and uploaded to the Internet, that substantiate this fact. One that does so is sanctioned by the organization that compiled the New Testament canon, the Catholic Church, from the *Original Encyclopedia*:

> But the genuine Gospels are silent about long stretches of the life of Our Lord, the Blessed Virgin, and St. Joseph. Frequently they give but a tantalizing glimpse of some episode on which we would fain be more fully informed. This reserve of the Evangelists did not satisfy the pardonable curiosity of many Christians eager for details, and the severe and dignified simplicity of their narrative left unappeased imaginations seeking the sensational and the marvelous. When, therefore, enterprising spirits responded to this natural craving by pretended Gospels full of romantic fables and fantastic and striking details, their fabrications were eagerly read and largely accepted as true by common folk who were devoid of any critical faculty and who were predisposed to believe what so luxuriously fed their pious curiosity. Both Catholics and Gnostics were concerned in writing these fictions. The former had no other motive than that of a pious fraud, being sometimes moved by a real though misguided zeal, as witness the author of the Pseudo-Matthew: Amcor Christi est cui satisfecimus. But the heretical apocryphists, while gratifying curiosity, composed spurious Gospels in order to trace backward their beliefs and peculiarities to Christ Himself (http://oce.catholic.com/index.php?title=Apocrypha).

The inference is, of course, that only those apocryphal books were corrupt, and that the canonized books were divinely preserved, error-free. But, as we will see, for the first four hundred year or so, the only difference in the divinity of those books was the doctrinal perception of the readers. The simple truth is that in the above statement we have a confession of tampering by the very institution that claims the Bible is the inspired and inerrant Word of God. Notice: "The former [the Catholic Church] had no motive other than that of a pious fraud." And who believed and accepted these false tales? "Common folk who were devoid of any critical faculty"— the ignorant, illiterate masses.

Pretended Gospels full of romantic fables and fantastically striking details: immaculate conceptions, manger scenes, singing angels, walking on water, resurrections from the dead. Exactly what we find in the Gospels—folktales written by "Common folk who were devoid of any critical faculty."

Numerous authors and theologians have tried to make a case for the originality of the New Testament by asserting that the books were written earlier than generally accepted, and that numerous copies from distant countries corroborate one another. They compare their validity with that of secular authors such as Plato, Suetonius, and Homer, whose works are acknowledged; and, of course, Paul, since his writings are recognized. Such reasoning might hold value if we had a copy from such an early date. However, our earliest New Testament copy, the Codex Sinaiticus, was written about 300 CE; therefore, it doesn't matter what was written three hundred years after Jesus—or twenty, or even five—because we have no proof of what was written at those early dates!

Of the four Gospels, Luke first came to light within the heretic Marcion's literature about 130-140 CE, and there is a debate as to whether Marcion rewrote the original Luke or not. Either instance would explain all the amazing new information about Jesus that Luke reveals to Theophilus—information not found in the earlier Gospels.

The Gospels are not mentioned nor referenced in any other works of the New Testament or secular writings until about 180 CE when Irenaeus refers to a defined set of four Gospels (*Irenaeus, Adversus Haereses, 3.11.8*).

Scholars suppose that Mark was composed in Rome or Antiochine Southern Syria, Matthew at Antioch, then part of Roman Syria, or in Northern Palestine, and Luke in a large city west of Palestine. Antioch was one of the largest cites of the Hellenist Jews of the Diaspora; Jews who had accepted Grecian values. They had also adopted much of Grecian mythology into their beliefs. This would account for Gentile nuances evidenced in the Gospels' locution.

Since we have proof that altering and rewriting Christian works was a common practice is there any reason we should not assume all the Gospels and Acts, as well as other canonical books might have been corrupted?

What of the Acts of the Apostles? Considered the second part of the Gospel of Luke, it was written between 80 & 90 CE by the same anonymous author. Therefore, though it might merit some historical and social value, it must share the same credibility as the Gospels.

As for the Gospel of John, that it was evidently written solely for the purpose of exalting Jesus' divinity denies its credibility.

⌒◦⊰❀⊱◦⌒

Paul was arrested about 57 CE. He spent the next two years awaiting trial before he was sent to Rome. How long he awaited Nero's pleasure is inconclusive as is his fate. Some speculate that he was executed about 68 CE. With his death there was an abrupt break in the details of the development of Christianity.

In 66 CE the Jewish War erupted in which the Jews slaughtered the Gentiles throughout Judea. The Gentiles then returned the favor with their own slaughter. Later, in 70 CE, Titus's scorched earth campaign decimated the Jews and destroyed the temple in Jerusalem. The last stronghold, Masada, fell in 73 CE. The temple and cites were razed, the people were slaughtered, both Jews and Gentiles, and all forms of government and organization were destroyed. Josephus' *Wars of the Jews*, reported the number of dead as 1,100,000 and 97,000 enslaved.

Josephus also described four religious groups in Judea: the Sadducees, the Pharisees, the Essenes, and the Zealots. The Sadducees were a priesthood associated with the Temple worship. The Pharisees were the keepers of the Law. The Essenes were pacifist groups that had withdrawn from society to await the Messiah. And the Zealots were fanatical rebels intent in driving the Romans out.

The destruction of the temple decentralized the ruling groups, the Sadducees and Pharisees. Without the temple, the Sadducees had no place to offer sacrifices and were soon lost in history. And though there are records of Jesus' Apostles, the Nazarines, preaching Christ the tales are highly unlikely. They were likely Essenes, and that group also fell from the pages of history. When the dust settled Jerusalem and the existing Jewish culture had been annihilated. The aftermath of this war helped differentiate Christianity as a religion distinct from Judaism.

In 130 CE, Hadrian ... rebuilt the city [Jerusalem] according to his own designs and renamed it Aelia Capitolina Jupiter Capitolinus after himself and the king of the Roman gods. When he built a temple to Jupiter on the ruins of the Temple of Solomon ... the populace rose up under the leadership of Simon bar Kochba ... in what has come to be known as the Bar-Kochba Revolt (132-136 CE). ... By the time the rebellion was put down, 580,000 Jews had been killed and over 1000 towns and villages destroyed. Hadrian then banished the remaining Jews from the region and renamed it Syria Palaestina after the traditional enemies of the Jewish people, the Philistines. He ordered a public burning of the Torah, executed the Jewish scholars, and prohibited the practice and observance of Judaism. - *Ancient History Encyclopedia*

Except for Paul's writings, all records of Christian history, along with those of the Essenes, Zealots, and Sadducees were destroyed or lost. Only the Pharisees were left to reformulate a new form of Jewish worship. It is in this social setting that we are to believe the Jewish Apostles were spreading the gentile gospel to a gentile world. History is written by the victors and the Gentiles were attempting to erase all traces of the Jews and their messiah from the face of the earth. No Messianic Jew would have preached Jesus Christ, so the messengers had to be Gentiles or Hellenistic Jews.

For a period of almost seventy years, from the conclusion of Paul's writings—about 57 CE until 130 CE—all records of the Christian Church ceased to exist. There were other Christian churches, groups who knew nothing of Jesus or his atoning sacrifice, and there were Christian writings but none give us a true picture of the development of the seven churches Paul established. It is supposed that the Gospels were written during this period, but the period of their tales only cover the life of Jesus. We have no idea what occurred during that seventy-year historical gap. When history resumes, we are introduced to a new religion, presumably through Paul's writings, but we have no idea how that religion evolved, only that it reappeared within historical and New Testament writings about 130 CE. And here we face another dilemma—that new religion did not reappear alone. When the historical window once again opens, we find not one Christian religion, but dozens, perhaps hundreds, of different sects all claiming to be Christians, and all teaching differing doctrines.

In the early second century, the works of men like Clement of Alexandria, Polycarp, Athengoras, Theophilus, and Justin Martyr began to appear. Don't misunderstand, there were many writings and authors from many different and varied philosophies and *Christian* groups. There was a deluge of conflicting doctrines and beliefs from splintered groups and sects professing all types of *Christian* beliefs. And among them, apologists like Theophilus of Antioch,

Athenagoras of Athens, Tatian, and Minucius Felix wrote letters and apologies to the senate and rulers pleading their case and describing the doctrines of their belief—**and they never mentioned Jesus or a redeeming savior! None defended a crucified and resurrected redeemer. None mentioned the Word as being incarnate or made flesh, in fact, some even ridiculed the idea of a man being god or that of worshiping a dead man.** Their mediator between man and god was the Logos, the Greek Word, and redemption came through obedience to the **Word of God—the Jewish Law.** Despite their lack of knowledge of Jesus, **some of those apologists were bishops in the Catholic Church, some became saints, and today, all are regarded as defenders of the faith by the Church!**

There were all types of letters, rebuttals, and apologies. Each group was destroying, altering, or refuting the others' writings. There was often violent contention over Christian doctrine and the historicity of events and people—there just wasn't any information concerning the development and growth of the Church. Is the Catholic Church, as we know it today, descended from Paul's Church? Most likely. As mentioned before, it teaches many doctrines that originated with Paul, but we really have no way of being sure.

Christians often think of those Jerusalem Nazarenes as Paul's Church, but it should be obvious that the Nazarenes, descendants of Jesus' Apostles, were still clinging to messianic hopes. The original Apostles and disciples were Jews who had been reared within the teachings of the Law and the Prophets. Those who followed and embraced Paul's teachings were either Hellenistic Jews or Gentiles with pagan backgrounds and little understanding of the Old Testament. Paul had established a number of churches, but all were outside Judea. Had there been any in Judea, following the Jewish-Gentile war and the destruction of Jerusalem, there were obviously no survivors left who were inclined to record what happened to a few Christians. Any such records would have been destroyed in the literary wars that occurred between the contending religious sects during the following centuries. And the Apostles certainly would not have written gospels advocating a gentile Jesus, which only reinforces the certainty that the authors were Hellenistic Jews.

Even at that early date, the fusion of different religions and confusion of conflicting doctrines was already producing many arguments that still persist today. Oral fables of Jesus and his Apostles had been incorporated within the teachings of Paul. The Apostles' efforts to get Paul to submit to the Jewish Law, one of the last actions recorded in the Acts of the Apostles, exhibited their opposition to Paul's teachings and their dedication to the Mosaic Law. But early second century writers, striving to build a foundation for their new religion, converted those long dead Apostles to Christianity. Remember, Paul's churches were in gentile cities outside Judea. Decades had passed since his death and the leadership of the churches had fallen to teachers and elders who had little knowledge of their new savior, his true message, or the customs of the Jewish people and their religion. And, Paul was no longer there to speak for the invisible and silent Jesus.

There were other opposing sects and philosophies and a constant struggle against Judaism, paganism, and heresy, meaning any belief other than their own. Oft times the contentions ended in suppression and persecutions for the Christians. Sects appeared, and vanished. Heresies arose and faded. One day's Christian might be tomorrow's heretic. The rebellion between Gentiles and Jews created a love/hate relationship between the two cultures. The Gentiles were captivated by the Jewish philosophy and were tied to the Jewish God, but the Jewish War had created a hatred that still smolders today. By the second century—after the New Testament literature was written—the term Christian was exclusively Gentile. There were messianic Jewish sects that recognized Jesus as their Messiah, such as the Nazarenes and Ebionites, but there were no Jews in the Christian churches. Christianity, from the beginning was a gentile religion, conceived by Paul and for the most part, written by Gentiles, for Gentiles. The Christian idea that the Jews had killed their savior labeled them as Christ-killers, and the term sprang from the hateful lips and pens of the Romans and early Christians.

The hostilities and persecutions that occurred between all these sects and philosophies were not localized incidents that flared up and ended with the demise of the participants. They were confrontations that would intensify and spread throughout the *civilized* world during the next fifteen hundred years. The most important point that should be noted is the diversity of Christian beliefs during this period in history. Those differences make it obvious that orthodox Christianity did not evolve straight and pure from Judaism, but was a bi-product of Hellenistic philosophy and Paul's teachings strained through nearly seven decades of religious and philosophical controversy. What transpired in those missing years (57-130 CE) is unknown to everyone except the Church, which claims the evolution of the Jewish Apostles into Christian Apostles. However, all we can be sure of is that Pauline Christianity appeared with the new century. The logical explanation is that few of the local leaders who stepped forward after Paul's death would have known the Apostles, other than by name. And since they were directly connected with Jesus, the Gentiles' savior, it would only be logical that fables attributed to them, should be Christianized and introduced into the Church.

Letters between the gentile churches became our New Testament Epistles. Pastorals were penned, and the Gospels composed from folktales, all espousing Christian values. There were many Christian sects based upon philosophy, Gnosticism, mystery cults, and Jesus movements—any one, or a combination, could have evolved into today's Christianity.

If we pause and consider the events that were unfolding, it becomes evident that we are unraveling the distillation of Christian doctrines. Religious leaders, probably in all good faith, were arguing for their concept of what God desired. Unlike God's personal delivery of the Law and Ten Commandments to Moses, Christians were left to their own devices. In all likelihood the very first Jesus sect leaders, working from Paul's letters and the Greek Septuagint, wrote their own epistles and doctrines, and provided their own interpretations. In some cases, the works were group efforts, and the resultant documents were unsigned until a later date, when an Apostles' name was affixed. And authors thought nothing of correcting or adding to others works.

To add credence to their own writings, those early Christians often looked around for authority, and like any good promotional agency, they turned to big name appeal. They would have had little knowledge of the Apostles, other than their names and the few references made to them by Paul, and even Paul would not have known them very well since they only met a few times. But the names were all those early Christians needed, because a student's writing was often considered an extension of the master's thoughts. So, with total conviction that they were speaking for Paul (or John, Peter, or James) they penned the name of an Apostle to their works. With that simple gesture they destroyed what the Romans could not—the identity of Jesus' Apostles and their dedication to the Law. With a few strokes of the pen, devout Jews were transformed into Christians, and lifetimes of sacrifice, practicing circumcision, and observing the Law were taken from them. Peter's disassociation from Paul and his refusal to meet with Cornelius was excused. And James, a Nazarite, the Oblias (Just) or Zaddik, the most revered holy man in all Judea who died proclaiming Jesus the Messiah, was converted to Christianity by some unknown author's fables. And why not—since Paul had resurrected a Christian Jesus, it was not only logical, but absolutely necessary that Jesus' disciples should also be Christians.

But it doesn't end there. As one congregation rose to dominance, it assumed the power and right to dictate the beliefs of others. For authority, it turned to its apostolic writings—those written by its own members and others it had carefully screened and collected—the more writings, the greater the authority. The writings of Paul provided the doctrinal foundation for the Church, but Paul's Jesus was a spirit, and, as we have seen, in real life had not taught Paul's brand of salvation. Of course, oral tradition was already fleshing out Jesus' character. This was the beginning of the orthodox or Catholic Church. When we consider the emphasis on apostolic writings, tradition, and the succession of teachers, it becomes evident that their teachings were modeled after schools of Greek philosophy—more evidence the writings were Hellenistic. Such schools were understood to have had a founder/teacher whose teachings were transmitted through a line of disciple/teachers known as successors (*diadochoi*). The teachings were known as *traditions*—the building blocks of Catholic doctrine today.

When the Church turned to referencing traditions as their authority during the middle of the second century, the purpose was not to accurately record and preserve the stories. By then, the truth concerning the life of Jesus, what he taught, his ministry, even the beginning of Christianity, had been bound up in a tapestry of fables. When early Church champions, such as Irenaeus and Tertullian, began arguing for Church traditions and a succeeding line of apostolic descent, there was no proof—only ambiguous and vague references handed down by oral tradition. To compound the problem, even those tales were confusing. For example, the names of the twelve disciples, as well as their authority, were questionable. As a matter of fact, the number twelve is ambiguous. The writer of

Mark made the first attempt to build a base for that authority when he had Jesus send the disciples out. Of course, that still didn't provide much information about them or their works. Matthew did better with the *great commission*, but it was Luke who rose to the occasion when he had a resurrected Jesus appear to the eleven, had them elect a replacement for Judas, celebrate Pentecost, and then through the Holy Spirit, sent them out to spread the gospel of truth (Acts 2). But those scrabbling to formulate a line of succession still had no stories of these disciples' works—thus the need for texts. Soon many were writing texts in the name of one disciple or another. Often they would be accompanied with stories of the disciple's acts, his missions, and teachings. Since many of these did not conform to Catholic teachings, most were destroyed.

⋰⋱

Today, Christians, especially Catholics, speak the names of the early Fathers, such as Irenaeus, Eusebius, Clement, Tertullian, and Augustine with reverent awe. They are upheld as the pillars of knowledge and holiness—and in a time of superstition and ignorance, perhaps they were. Education was limited to the clergy, with the focus being on Church propaganda rather than reason. The Church Fathers' agenda was to prove and promote Church doctrines, not to uncover *truth*. Paul had already furnished them with the truth. Their goal was to connect all the gaping contradictions and mold that *truth* into a believable, though senseless, story.

Outside New Testament Scriptures, the Church observed many customs and traditions declared divine simply because they were allegedly practiced by the early Church. Two examples are the veneration of Sunday as the Lord's Day and infant baptism. It should be noted that the early Church did not observe a Sunday Sabbath until it was instituted by Constantine in 321 CE. Decrees concerning the souls of unbaptized infants were still being passed in the eleventh century. But the most astounding ability allegedly given to the Church was the *tradition* that the Apostles were endowed with the ability to propagate "revealed truth" to their disciples—a doctrine referred to as apostolic succession. Stated bluntly, Catholicism claimed the divine right to speak for God. For authority, they turned to New Testament Scriptures (which they sanctioned) as a basis for this teaching. However, that interpretation isn't valid.

The fallacy of using tradition in this manner to support a religious dogma is that we must consider that all societies and religions have traditions. Recognizing one as authoritative, without any basis of validity, gives precedence to all the others to make like claims. Therefore, the Native American's tradition that man came from a hole in the earth is just as valid as that of the creation story— or Jesus rising from the grave.

None of the Catholic traditions were even recognized as divine until the orthodox Church began searching for preeminence over other Christian sects during the second century. The search for authoritative writings led the Church to concoct the theory of apostolic succession. Prior to that "revealed truth," traditions were used as a teaching method, or were simply customs.

Today, most Christian denominations teach the concept of apostolic succession, by which Jesus sent his disciples to preach salvation throughout the world. The commission is given in the Gospel of Matthew and was supposedly initiated on the day of Pentecost (Acts 2), but that simply cannot be true. Why? To answer that question we must first understand just how the Catholic Church defines the term *apostolic succession*, or apostolicity:

> Apostolicity of mission means that the Church is one moral body, possessing the mission entrusted by Jesus Christ to the Apostles, and transmitted through them and their lawful successors in an unbroken chain to the present representatives of Christ upon earth. This authoritative transmission of power in the Church constitutes apostolic succession. This apostolic succession must be both material and formal; the material consisting in the actual succession in the Church, through a series of persons from the Apostolic age to the present; the formal adding the element of authority in the transmission of power. It consists in the legitimate transmission of the ministerial power conferred by Christ upon His Apostles. No one can give a power which he does not possess. Hence in tracing the mission of the Church back to the Apostles, no lacuna can be allowed, no new mission can arise; but the mission conferred by Christ must pass from generation to generation through an uninterrupted lawful succession. The Apostles received it from Christ and gave it in turn to those legitimately appointed by them, and these again selected others

to continue the work of the ministry. Any break in this succession destroys Apostolicity, because the break means the beginning of a new series which is not Apostolic https://www.ecatholic2000. com/cathopedia/vol1/volone861.shtml.

Paramount to this tenet is the assertion that Peter was the first Bishop of Rome, but what proof can the Church present to support this claim and all that it implies? It all hinges upon the theory that Peter taught and died in Rome. Surely, there is concrete evidence to support that claim. The proof, as presented in the Catholics' *Original Encyclopedia:*

> It is an indisputably established historical fact that St. Peter laboured in Rome during the last portion of his life, and there ended his earthly course by martyrdom. As to the duration of his Apostolic activity in the Roman capital, the continuity or otherwise of his residence there, the details and success of his labours, and the chronology of his arrival and death, all these questions are uncertain, and can be solved only on hypotheses more or less well-founded. The essential fact is that Peter died at Rome : this constitutes the historical foundation of the claim of the Bishops of Rome to the Apostolic Primacy of Peter. https:// www.ecatholic2000.com/cathopedia/vol11/voleleven709.shtml

Doesn't it seem odd that the Church has "indisputably established historical fact," concerning Peter's martyrdom, and thereby his presence in Rome, yet it can present no evidence to support that claim. Observe the double talk. The Church has no idea how long Peter was in Rome or where he lived, no details of his works, no timetable as to when he arrived or died—only "hypotheses more or less well-founded." What does "more or less well-founded" mean? A statement can either be proven or not—it is either an established fact or a hypothesis. How then, can the Church state emphatically that: "The essential fact is that Peter died at Rome."? The Catholic Church presents this *indisputable proof* in two, vague, New Testament references and eleven historical allusions to those references (see reference above). The first refers us to John 21:18-19, where Jesus allegedly spoke to Peter:

> Verily, verily, I say unto thee. When thou wast young, thou girdedst thyself, and walkedst whither thou wouldest; but when thou shalt be old, thou shalt stretch forth thy hands, and another

shall gird thee, and carry thee whither thou wouldest not." This
spake he, signifying by what death he should glorify God.

In the first place, the Gospel of John is nothing more than a
spurious piece of propaganda written to glorify the manufactured
deification of Jesus. It can't even be harmonized with the other
Gospels, and was apparently considered insignificant until the latter
part of the second century. Regarding the interpretation of the
passage, I see no mention of Rome or martyrdom. What death does
it signify? That someone is going to grab Peter's garment and drag
him to death? I see no indication of crucifixion. In fact, it sounds
more like a promise of longevity—an old man who has to be dressed
and led about. There is no proof in this passage.

The second reference is to I Peter, which was "almost
undoubtedly" written from Rome. This dubious supposition,
coupled with the fact the Church can't even prove authorship of I
Peter, already gives it a shaky start. The passage in question is from
the closing address:

The church that is at Babylon, elected together with you, saluteth
you; and so does Marcus my son (I Peter 5:13).

"... so does Marcus my son." What should we infer from this?
If the author was Peter, was he referring to his companion, Mark,
as his son? Did Peter have a son named Marcus? Or, was the true,
unknown author of I Peter referring to his *own* son?

The Church deduced that since two of the four historical
"Babylon" cities were destroyed and Jerusalem was in ruins, it had
to be Rome.

First, notice that both of these passages, which are supposed
to be the basis for one of the most important tenets of Christianity,
are only vague metaphors. Why would Jesus, or Peter, use such
ambiguous statements as the only proof to establish the authority of
God's Church? Why didn't Jesus state plainly that Peter must preach
in Rome if the passage was to be so significant? Why didn't the writer
of I Peter just say Rome? And why would a Christian refer to Rome
as Babylon, when he would know the term referred to the "Mother
of harlots," and inferred an apostate church?

Babylon is not only used in reference to certain cities (or the
Mother of harlots), it is also used allegorically to indicate a state of

confusion, captivity, and the epitome of evil. Could the writer be implying he was a prisoner in a religious cult? Or, might the author be writing from Jerusalem, one of those three cites rejected as not being the Babylon in question? Since it is believed that I Peter was written prior to 110 CE, couldn't the Apostles have been reunited, with Peter still in residence. Though in all probability he was dead long before I Peter was written. And wouldn't the Babylon label be more appropriate for a devastated city, such as Jerusalem would have been?

All of this, together with the Church's assertion, is only speculation, and I don't believe either conjecture. At any rate, whatever conclusion is reached, this salutary remark is far from "indisputably established historical fact." So neither passage is conclusive.

Without New Testament proof, we're left with the eleven historical references which were drawn from the two refuted passages, and those are simply remarks based upon tradition. The first of the eleven references was presented by living witnesses— Papias of Hierapolis and Clement of Alexandria. Both men presented hearsay evidence that Mark wrote his Gospel in Rome, at the request of Roman Christians who wanted a memorial of Peter. Papias, who lived in the early second century, was allegedly only a generation removed from John the Apostle. Clement died in the early third century, so it's most likely Clement referenced a saying of Papias. And as we have already discovered, Papias' quotations were without validity. He would repeat anything told him without bothering to check its authenticity. It appears this evidence was also recorded by Irenaeus (middle second century) and copied by Eusebius about 330 CE—most likely from Clement. Now we shall see how the Catholic Church takes a splinter and builds a tree. From the same *Original Encyclopedia* source:

> Concerning the Gospel of St. Mark, Eusebius, relying perhaps on an earlier source, says that Peter described Rome figuratively as Babylon in his First Epistle.
> https://www.ecatholic2000.com/cathopedia/vol11/voleleven709.shtml

An "earlier source"—Papias? And we're back to that little reference to Babylon in I Peter 5:13. Here we find later writers starting to reference an offhand, vague remark in a closing address, written by an unknown author as absolute fact. From here, Catholics down through the ages have built upon this remark to prove what they **have** to establish—that Peter was the first Pope. Such is the foundation the Catholic Church is built upon—blocks of vague statements and lies, with faith and blood used as mortar. "Traditions of the presbyters" and "ecclesiastical tradition," because they survived for ages, unlike fairy tales, became *proof*. "Generally agreed" remarks and "acknowledged writings" became *facts*. Assertions of infallibility spoke for God, because few disputed the claim and lived. And, as we have seen here, vague references and gossip became "indisputably established historical fact."

So far, the best evidence presented to support the Church's claim is only inference and most likely only gossip—certainly not proof. As a matter of fact, if there was a Peter in Rome, how can we be sure he wasn't an impostor? How many people in Rome would have known Peter the Apostle? What credentials would he have needed?

There is really no need to investigate the evidence of the remaining ten reports because they present no new information. They are only ambiguous comments inspired by the two New Testament references, generally praising and glorifying Peter and Paul. (If the reader should wish to view those references they may be found at the website: https://www.ecatholic2000.com/cathopedia/vol11/voleleven709.shtml/.

Although the Catholic Church had been teaching apostolic succession for decades to gain preeminence over other *heretical* groups, the succession was not apostolic, but a claim for truth. Truth was the question—the claim to be the one true church. (See: Irenaeus, *Against Heresies* I:10:2; III:3:2; III:3:4; Tertullian, *Prescription Against Heretics* 21,36) To argue that apostolic succession has faithfully and accurately preserved apostolic tradition for two thousand years, including throughout the massively corrupt Middle Ages further denies such an assertion.

The actual term, apostolic succession wasn't used until after Constantine gained power and wanted to establish the Church's Papal authority in the Western Church—Rome. Note the last sentence in the OCE quote above concerning Peter in Rome. *The essential fact is that Peter died at Rome:* **this constitutes the historical foundation of the claim of the Bishops of Rome to the Apostolic Primacy of**

Peter. Constitutes the historical foundation—what the Church is built upon.

We could further contest the evidence for the Church's assertion by referring to the accumulation of contradictions found throughout the New Testament, but that would be like attempting to dam a river as it enters the sea. Instead, we'll simply go to the source and point out the fact that in the year 58 CE, approximately twenty years after the crucifixion (Acts 21), the Apostles were not teaching Paul's (nor Jesus') Christian doctrines. Instead, they were attempting to confirm Paul's belief in the Law. Even so, the Catholic Church tries to depict the Apostles, in Acts and Galatians, as back-sliding, judaizing Christians:

> The first council was a meeting of the Apostles at Jerusalem in order to put an end to the judaizing tendencies among the first Christians https://www.ecatholic2000.com/cathopedia/vol7/volseven300.shtml

Notice how they have twisted the context. Instead of Paul's teaching against circumcision being under question it's the "judaizing Christians" who are in error. The *Catholic Encyclopedia* completely disregards the fact that those "judaizing Christians" were not Christians at all, but the chosen Apostles of Jesus, Messianic Jews. When historians and theologians speak of Christian Jews they are unknowingly referring to Nazarenes, Ebionites, or Hellenistic Messianic Jewish sects. The idea that there were Jewish Christians when Rome and the Christian world were killing and persecuting them as Christ-killers is unimaginable.

I've already referred to the passage in Gal. 2:11, where Paul rebuked Peter, and mentioned secular writers such as Hippolytus (Circa 215 CE) and Eusebius (Circa 325 CE) who claimed Peter and other Apostles were preaching Jesus Christ in various countries such as Galatia, Cappadocia, Asia, and Rome. Admittedly, this does give strong evidence for the Christianization of Jesus' Apostles. But it does not explain the obvious contradiction that those Apostles were keeping the Law when they were last mentioned in the New Testament. Neither can it stand as proof that Jesus commissioned them to preach salvation to the Gentiles, for even if the twelve had converted to Christianity, they could not have done so until after the chronological ending of the New Testament. Meaning, they would have been following Paul's mission, not the command of Jesus, thereby breaking the "transmission of the ministerial power conferred by Christ upon his Apostles," and the mediation of a new covenant (Heb. 9:15-17).

The clergy of the Catholic Church spent over 100 years arguing and literally fighting before agreeing as to what should be included within the New Testament. They searched for and examined every gospel, epistle, or work that could possibly be connected to Jesus or his followers—all in the hopes of proving their theory of apostolic succession. And the best they could find were the two ambiguous statements just examined. Surely, if such a speculation were true there would have been numerous instances in the Acts of the Apostles and many of the other writings were the apostles were doing so. Instead, we can find only two instances: that of Peter at Cornelius' and Phillip and the Ethiopian—both obvious interpolations.

You simply cannot uphold Church traditions without discrediting the New Testament, because the Scriptures teach the opposite of the tradition. You are faced with the choice of either denouncing tradition, or labeling the New Testament as false. And if you denounce the traditions, then you must admit to interpolations within the New Testament. This is the reason the Catholic Church strives so hard to enroll Peter within their fold. He **has** to be the link that connects Paul's *new religion* to the faith of Jesus. However, Peter's role in the matter is minimal, to say the least. It should be noted that Catholicism did not make the claim of apostolic succession until the fourth century—three hundred years after the *foundation* was laid. The Church's rise to power came first, and then the authoritative claim for the right to rule.

But what of Peter's speech on the day of Pentecost, when he preached salvation through Christ? This is one of the main passages the Catholic Church uses to *prove* that Peter had converted to Christianity, and that he was performing the commission Jesus supposedly gave to the Apostles following his resurrection. And yet, later passages in the New Testament show that Peter was still observing the Law: when he told Cornelius that it was unlawful for a Jew to consort with Gentiles (Acts 10:28), when he separated from Paul's gentile converts (Galatians 2:12), and he was standing with the Apostles and is identified as a leader of the Apostles at the council with Paul (Galatians 2:9).

If close consideration is given to these events, attempts to undermine Peter's dedication to the Law are evident. For example, when he showed loyalty to the Law by questioning Cornelius' intentions, the vision of unclean beasts was introduced. When he separated from the Gentiles, he was rebuked by Paul. And when he stood with the Apostles at the council, the writer of Luke (or perhaps a later editor) inserted a scene in which Peter pleaded on Paul's behalf (Acts 15:7-11). In that plea, Peter claimed God chose him to preach to the Gentiles (verse 7) and James seconded that assertion (verse 14).

This is all very confusing. Let's see: Peter received the commission to preach to the Gentiles from a risen Jesus (Acts 10:40-43), Then on Pentecost, he preached a rousing sermon that touched the hearts of three thousand souls. However, despite such a miraculous work, he couldn't figure out how he was to preach to the Gentiles without associating with them. So, God gave him a vision which led him to Cornelius and the outpouring of the Holy Ghost upon the Gentiles. Then, with a confident mind, he attended the Jerusalem Council and declared God's calling. James agreed with Peter's claim. However, Paul said: "No, Peter's gospel is to the circumcision; I was called to the Gentiles" (Galatians 2:7-8). Poor Peter; later, when he went to Antioch, he didn't know what to do. Paul had him so confused he didn't even know if he was to eat with the Gentiles or not (Galatians 2:11-12). Tell me, does this sound like the image of a pope, a man capable of transmitting the ecclesiastical tradition and the preaching of the truth?

And what was the "gospel of the circumcision" that Peter was to preach? Do you think, perhaps, he was to tell the Jews they didn't have to be circumcised, or that the Law was rendered null through Jesus Christ? Of course not, he was a Messianic Jew, he was teaching Jews, and he was teaching them the same message Jesus taught—the coming kingdom of God. What was the Jerusalem Council about? The Apostles were trying to get Paul to support the Law. And none of them were teaching salvation through Jesus. It's very unlikely that any of the Apostles had ever heard of a commission to the Gentiles until Paul started his ministry.

All of these unsubstantiated incidents were created to associate Peter with Paul's teachings, but they cannot be harmonized within the New Testament Scriptures. These are direct contradictions, with the continuity so conflicting as to be ridiculous. Something Christian faith refuses to see, and a choice must be made between them. The simplest way to do that is to compare the speaker's concept of the Law to the events depicted. For example, in Peter's case; he was an Apostle and a member of the messianic Jews in Jerusalem. He kept the Law. Obviously, Jesus did not teach him differently. Therefore, he would not preach salvation through Jesus. The same can be said for the other Apostles. As for Jesus: he died for that belief, and taught obedience to the Law throughout his ministry. How can we be sure? His Apostles continued to teach and observe the Law after his death, proving that Jesus did not teach salvation through a Christian belief in his resurrection. On the other hand, Paul is the only identifiable figure in the entire New Testament who preached salvation through Jesus Christ, and did not keep the Law.

~❧~

The Church pointed to old traditions and introduced new ones as she aged. Since she alone claimed the right of apostolic succession, those ecclesiastical traditions gave her magisterial power to decide what was "revealed truth." In effect, that absolute power gave the Church leaders license to institute whatever dogma was needed to further the gospel of Christ, and therefore, their will.

Eusebius was the first historian to write a history of the Christian Church, completed about 327 CE at the height of Constantine's power. However, it should be noted that it was a Church history, as opposed to a national history. Its purpose was to refute Gnosticism by establishing the line of apostolic succession, and thereby, the authority of the Church. In actuality, no one had bothered to keep a history of the Church prior to Eusebius. So, whatever he wrote, be it factual or fraudulent, became the official history of the Catholic Church. Richard Carrier, B.A., M.A., M. Phil., Ph. D., states in his *The Formation of the New Testament Canon (2000)* that Eusebius was either a liar or hopelessly credulous, and not a good historian. He also pointed out that Eusebius had to have rewritten his *History of the Church* at least five times to accommodate changing events.

When it came to choosing the texts for canonization, Eusebius first accepted every book recognized by every orthodox author he knew. The next category was chosen from those generally recognized, but disputed by at least someone—someone he regarded as orthodox, which eliminated early church leaders like Marcion. The final selection included those universally rejected as heretical by those who accepted his idea of orthodoxy. The problems with this process should be obvious: first, it begins with his own judgment of authenticity—whose opinion counts at all. Secondly, it is based solely on the doctrinal opinions of these writers. There is no standard of research or textual criticism.

Another great weakness of many early Church writers, bishops, and Fathers—including Tertullian, Justin Martyr, and even St. Augustine—was that they believed that the old pagan gods were real. Also, many early Christian Fathers, including Athenagoras and Justin Martyr, quoted from the pagans' Sibyline Oracles. Most early Christian Church leaders and theologians were converted Greek pagans who continued to believe in the reality of the pagan gods. However, many did recognize them as false gods and Satan's demons. And as the pagan tales were incorporated into Christianity and attributed to Jesus, the originals were claimed to be counterfeits by Satan, who could foresee the coming events and created his own false religions to discredit and cast doubt upon the truth. Many also believed in magic and astrology. They were attuned and receptive to miracles such as healings, magic tricks, and divinations. The actuality of such magic was not questioned, only the power, whether it be good or evil—of god or the devil. The truthfulness of a prophet's message wasn't judged so much by reason and logic as by the power of the prophet. This is a truth that may be traced back throughout secular history and the annals of Israel. Consider the stories of Moses, Joshua, Elijah, and Daniel. Even Paul referenced "… signs, in wonders, and mighty deeds" as proof of his ministry (II Corinthians 12:12). There were specific reasons for this evaluation method. The main culprit was ignorance, fostered by a lack of education and readily available information. Reason was tossed aside in favor of human emotionalism—or mysticism. But we should not lose sight of the fact that the entire world during the first century was shrouded in miracles, magic and superstitions. Even the educated Greek and Roman philosophers offered sacrifices to appease the gods, and no emperor or ruler would dare make an important state decision without consulting an oracle. Why doesn't it amaze me that one word you won't find in the Bible is hallucinating though it is, and was a common occurrence?

When one reads the writings of the early Church leaders and champions, the most obvious facet is that of contention, not only with differing factions, but also within their own ranks. There was a constant power struggle for favorable diocese or providence, and arguments over doctrines and interpretations of scriptures. The professed reason was to protect the newly converted heathen from the heretics, with a heretic being defined as anyone who disagreed with *their* Church doctrine, but the main reason was because more writings equated to a more meaningful orthodoxy. All this led to the evolution of a canon of New Testament writings toward the end of the third century, where their authority was declared by the men who ran it. For more information see Paul Johnson's, *A History of Christianity*, (Part 1, pp 54-56).

⸗⸒

In the spring of 312 CE, the Roman Empire was in a state of upheaval. In the East, the old Caesar was dying and Christians were the subjects of designed, imperial extermination. In the West, the Emperor Constantine was marching against Rome and his rival, Maxentius. Constantine was outnumbered. He faced the prospect of attacking a fortified city where his foe's position was more strategic. Also, Constantine believed Maxentius was the possessor of a strong magical enchantment. As a worshiper of the sun, the *Sol Invictus*, Constantine knew he needed some counter magic. What occurred next has been published in countless books. Almost every Christian is familiar with Constantine's vision, which he described as a cross glowing in the sky with the words, "by this sign you will be victor." This event supposedly led him to the Christian God. (Isn't it interesting how personal visions are so readily accepted as divine proof?) Whether or not Constantine truly experienced a vision has been the subject of much debate but for whatever reason, he credited the Christian God for his success in defeating his rival and attaining the throne. It appears that the same superstitious fear that led him to seek a sign also drove him to champion the Catholic Church, and in turn, pave the way for Christianity to become the state religion.

Apparently, Constantine was terrified of losing God's favor, and thus his throne, for whenever he perceived a threat against the

Christians he personally took steps to rectify the situation. In 313 CE, he issued the Edict of Milan, which proclaimed official toleration of the Christian faith. Later, that toleration was extended to favorite status, and finally, Christianity was the only recognized religion. One of Constantine's first acts was to put the clergy on the state payroll, thereby buying their loyalty and negating voluntary contributions as decreed by Paul. Next, he donated a large private estate to Miltiades, the Bishop of Rome, and lured him and his successors away from Jesus' disdain for riches. He rebuilt the churches that had been destroyed during recent persecutions. Exiles were allowed to return and their property was restored. Special monetary gifts were given to the families of martyrs and those who "confessed Christ." (In other words, he bought converts.) And he sent letters to the Eastern Emperors imploring them to cease persecution of the Christians. Because of the dissensions between the various Christian sects, he stepped in and dictated a settlement. When the problem persisted, he proclaimed the Catholic Church the only Church and declared all others heretic.

His zeal for, and fear of, the Christian God was so great that he did everything possible to appease his new deity—short of accepting baptism. The affects upon the Church were like the unleashing of an evil plague that spread throughout Christendom. By his actions and decrees, he usurped the power, traditions, customs, and rituals of the Catholic Church, and rebuilt it upon the principles of the Roman Empire. He laid the building blocks of the Holy Roman Empire, even though that state would not be recognized until 800 CE.

Prior to this time, all Christians, whether Catholic, Marcionite, Montanist, or Gnostic, had looked forward to the Day of Judgment, when their Savior, Jesus Christ, would return and destroy the Romans and all who did not confess Jesus' name. Imagine the confusion within the Christian world when Rome suddenly did an about-face and became their protector and benefactor. Considering the Church's belief that all rulers were ordained by God, is it any wonder they believed Constantine had been elevated to that role? He was certainly championing their cause. And when he began using all means available to destroy the wickedness of the pagans, what else could Christians do but embrace this unexpected gift from heaven?

And so it was that the spiritual warriors yielded to the secular designs of Constantine.

⌐⊂✿⊃⌐

By the end of the third century, the Catholic Church no longer comprised scattered conclaves of persecuted groups. They had long before begun to attract the wealthy and intelligent. They were organized with their own dioceses and seats of government, their own clergy, and influential leaders. In many cases, because they were outlawed, they had avoided taxation. That, plus over two hundred years of passing wealth on in perpetuity had given them financial power. A hundred years before (c. 200 CE), Tertullian had written that they were numerous enough to overthrow the Empire:

> We are but of yesterday, and we fill everything you have—cities, tenements, forts, towns, exchanges, yes! And camps, tribes, palace, senate, forum. All we leave you with are the Temples! For what wars should we not be fit, not eager, even with unequal forces, we who so willingly yield ourselves to the sword, if in our religion it were not counted better to be slain than to slay? Without arms even, and raising no insurrectionary banner, but simply in enmity to you, we could carry on the contest with you by an ill-willed severance alone. For if such multitudes of men were to break away from you, and betake themselves to some remote corner of the world, why, the very loss of so many citizens, whatever sort they were, would cover the empire with shame; nay, in the very forsaking, vengeance would be inflicted. Why, you would be horror-struck at the solitude in which you would find yourselves, at such an all-prevailing silence, and that stupor as of a dead world. You would have to seek subjects to govern. You would have more enemies than citizens remaining. For now it is the immense number of Christians which makes your enemies so few, almost all the inhabitants of your various cities being followers of Christ (*Apology*, Chap. 37.326).

Throughout all Christendom, much has been publicized of Christians being executed or tossed to the lions. Such tales were highly exaggerated; most of those tossed to the lions were criminals, prisoners of war, or deserters from the army. True, from the second and into the fourth century—prior to Constantine—

there were persecutions of Christians. At times, they were reviled, discriminated against, and forced to recant or else suffer torture and death. However, most often such persecutions came from within their own ranks, from rival sects, or from the local populace. There was no systematic, government persecution before the second half of the second century. The worst episodes were isolated incidents, or occurred under weak and vulnerable rulers such as Nero, Domitian, Septimus Severus, and Diocletian. For the most part, Rome accepted Christianity as another religion. They were left alone, so long as they caused no trouble. They did not hide in the catacombs, to do so would have conflicted with their faith. Tertullian, considered one of the greatest Church writers, and the first to introduce Latin works, says they identified themselves:

> At every forward step and movement, at every going in and out, when we put on our clothes and shoes, when we bathe, when we sit at table, when we light the lamps, on couch, on seat, in all the ordinary actions of daily life, we trace upon out forehead the sign of the cross (De Corona).

And from the *First Apology* of Justin Martyr:

> And reckon ye that it is for your sakes we have been saying these things; for it is in our power, when we are examined, to deny that we are Christians; but we would not live by telling a lie. For, impelled by the desire of the eternal and pure life, we seek the abode that is with God, the Father and Creator of all, and hasten to confess our faith, persuaded and convinced as we are that they who have proved to God by their works that they followed Him, and loved to abide with Him where there is no sin to cause disturbance, can obtain these things.

Certain sects of the early Christians were fanatical in their beliefs, and as a number of writers have stated, "zealous for death," that they might be with their Lord.

Even though Constantine labored diligently in his new God's behalf, he obviously saw the potential opportunities offered by a union with such a group—plus the consequences that resistance could eventually bring to pass. He put his civil power behind the Church and became one of the greatest authors in the annals of Christianity. As their champion, he was accepted greedily, blindly, and without reservation. In 323 CE, Constantine summoned the first General Council of the Church at Nicea.

> The Emperor himself presided, "like some heavenly messenger of God," as one of those present, Eusebius, Bishop of Caesarea, expressed it. At the conclusion of the council the bishops dined with the Emperor. "The circumstances of the banquet," wrote Eusebius (who was inclined to be impressed by such things), "were splendid beyond description. Detachments of the bodyguard and other troops surrounded the entrance of the palace with drawn swords, and through the midst of these men of God proceeded without fear into the innermost of the imperial apartments. Some were the Emperor's own companions at table, others reclined on couches ranged on either side. One might have thought it was a picture of Christ's kingdom, and a dream rather than reality." (Bishop Kallistos Ware, *The Orthodox Church*).

Eusebius was the nominal host, and one of three prominent Church leaders at the Council of Nicea. From the beginning, Constantine took control and directed the proceedings. Because of his support for Arianism, Eusebius was asked to validate his orthodoxy by giving his confession of faith. After he did so, Constantine asked him point blank if he could accept the term *homoousios*, "of one substance," to explain the relationship between the Father and Son. Eusebius caved-in and denied Arianism. From that moment on, the council was Constantine's and Eusebius was his boot-licker. For the rest of his life, Eusebius worked incessantly to integrate the Church within Roman administrative guidelines.

But what type of person was Constantine and what contributions did he make to the growth and stability of the Church? Erich Von Daniken, in *Miracles Of The Gods*, enlightens us.

> It all began with the councils, the assemblies of ecclesiastical senior pastors for dealing with important ecclesiastical affairs. A prerequisite for the appointment of an official of the Church is that he have "charisma," i.e., that he share the "divine gift of grace." So, when councils with such illustrious members meet, the Holy Ghost is among them, omnipresent and active.
>
> The Assemblies of the first five Ecumenical (which means the whole Catholic Church) Councils of the early Christian world

set the standards for the doctrine and organization of the new religion.

The oldest dogmas, which are still valid today, were proclaimed at Nicaea (AD 325), Constantinople (381), Ephesus (431), Chalcedon (451), and again at Constantinople (553). It is worthwhile to pause for a minute and take a quick look at how the Councils came into being and what decisions were made by them—presumably for all eternity.

The first Ecumenical Council took place at Nicaea. The Council was convened by the Emperor Constantine (who was not crowned until he was on his deathbed), because he wanted to use the rapidly expanding Christian religion, with its great potentialities, to strengthen the Roman Empire. When Constantine selected and brought together the 318 bishops for the Council, it was pure power politics, religious concerns taking very much of a back seat. Even the charismatic bishops can have had no doubt about that, for not only did the Emperor preside over the council, he also expressly proclaimed that his will was ecclesiastical law. The senior pastors accepted him as "Universal Bishop," even though he was uncrowned, and they let him take part in votes on Church dogmas as a secular prince. Ecclesiastical and earthly interests entered into an astonishing symbiosis even at that early stage!

Constantine was completely ignorant of Jesus' teaching. He was a follower of the solar cult of Mithras (ancient Iranian god of light), who was portrayed on coins as the "invincible sun" and worshiped until far into the Christian era. When Constantine gave his name to the old Greek commercial city of Byzantium and made Constantinople (330) the capital of the Roman Empire, he had a mighty column erected for the ceremonial opening of the metropolis with the Emperor and the invincible sun on top of it, forgetting all about Christian humility. Clouds of incense floated in the air, and candlelit processions made their tortuous way through the streets in his honor. Far from abolishing slavery, in the Christian spirit of loving one's neighbor, the Pontifex ordered that slaves caught pilfering food have molded lead poured down their throats, and he allowed parents to sell their children in times of need.

What were the ecclesiastical/political decisions that this emperor had a hand in?

Until Nicaea, the doctrine of Arius of Alexandria that God and Christ were not identical, but only similar, held good. Constantine forced the Council to proclaim that God the Father and Jesus were of the same essence. This absolutely vital amendment became Church dogma by imperial decree. That is how Jesus became identical with God. With this as a foundation, the bishops unanimously passed the 'Nicene Creed.'

The non-Christian Constantine did the Church another enormous service. Until that time, the place where Jesus was buried had remained unknown. Then, in the year of grace 326, the Roman Emperor, led by "divine inspiration," discovered the grave of Jesus, who had just become consubstantial with God. (In 330 Constantine had the Church of the Holy Sepulcher built.) However, this wonderful discovery did not stop Constantine from murdering some of his close relatives during the same year: his son Crispus; his wife, Faustina, whom he had plunged into boiling water; and his father-in-law, Maximian, whom he imprisoned and forced to commit suicide.

That is the image of the Emperor and Pontifex who stage-managed the Nicene Creed and who, when the council was over, told the Christian communities in a circular letter that the agreement of the 318 bishops was the "Decision of God" (*Miracles of the Gods*, Chap. 2, pp. 44-46).

Stop and ask yourself—if Jesus was recognized as the son of God as early as the first century, when Paul was writing, why did it take nearly three hundred years, and the intervention of a secular Emperor, for a spirit-led Church to determine Jesus' exact relationship with God? The answer is obvious: the decision did not come from the Church, but from Constantine. The Church leaders were so convinced that Constantine was empowered by God they surrendered all control to him.

Such reasoning became Church doctrine in the ensuing centuries as the Emperor was recognized as the head of the secular kingdom of God, while the pope was recognized as the God-ordained head of the spiritual Church. Taking their lead from Constantine, the emperors who succeeded him also made their contributions to the Church. Von Daniken continues:

The second Ecumenical Council was at Constantinople. This council was convened by the Emperor Theodosius I (347-395), who was flatteringly nicknamed 'the Great' by the Church. This Roman Emperor did not lag behind his colleague Constantine in moral qualities. He was an open oppressor of the poor, history tells us. He swamped the common people with intolerable burdens, which his tax collectors exacted with brutal tortures. With the full rigor of his imperial power, he forbade anyone to give refuge to these downtrodden creatures. If they did so, he had all the inhabitants of the offending village slaughtered. In the year 390 (almost ten years after the holy council) he had seven thousand rebellious citizens murdered in a frightful bloodbath in the center of the town of Thessalonika—at the same time that the 'Halleluya' ('Praise Jehovah') came into use in Christian churches. Theodosius proclaimed the Christian doctrine the state religion (hence 'the Great') and made Ambrosius, Bishop of Milan, level all heathen sanctuaries to the ground. With his methods, Theodosius could well have been the ancestor of the Inquisition. If Jesus preached a joyous message to the poor and oppressed, Theodosius was Antichrist in person. Yet this Unholy Ghost convened the second Council at Constantinople.

What happened there?

The dogma of the trinity of Father, Son, and Holy Ghost was introduced into Church doctrine. This was done by the assembly of senior pastors known by theological experts as the Rump Council. It was turned into the 'Niceno-Constantinopolitan Creed.' And—something for connoisseurs of the finer points of theology—the consubstantiality (of Nicaea) now became the identity of Father, Son, and Holy Ghost. Today the Church still feeds on the dogma of the Trinity that was added in this way (*Miracles of the Gods*, Chap. 2, pp. 46-47).

Constantine was only the first of a long line of emperors who built the Church up to the greatest religious power the world has ever seen, a power that crushed nations and dictated to kings. But their true colors became evident with the atrocities of Theodosius the Great (11 January 347 – 17 January 395). Under his reign, reason and knowledge were crucified to the god of faith, and the entire Christian world began sliding into the Dark Agess of ignorance. The pre-Nicene Christians looked to the power of God, and the seed of their martyrdom, to perpetuate the Church; after the authority was handed over to Constantine at the Council of Nicea, the spreading of the gospel was placed in the hands of secular power.

The characteristics, however, of the pre-Constantinian hierarchy, in distinction from the post-Constantinian, both Greek and Roman, are, first, its grand simplicity, and secondly, its spirituality, or freedom from all connection with political power and worldly splendor. Whatever influence the church acquired and exercised, she owed nothing to the secular government, which continued indifferent or positively hostile till the protective toleration edict of Constantine (313).

Tertullian thought it impossible for an emperor to be a Christian, or a Christian to be an emperor; and even after Constantine, the Donatists persisted in this view, and cast up to the Catholics the memory of the former age: "What have Christians to do with kings? Or what have bishops to do in the palace?" The ante-Nicene fathers expected the ultimate triumph of Christianity over the world from a supernatural interposition at the second Advent. Origen seems to have been the only one in that age of violent persecution who expected that Christianity, by continual growth, would gain the dominion over the world (*History of the Christian Church*, Philip Shaff).

Prior to Constantine's Edict of Milan, whenever the Christians were persecuted they cried foul and wrote apologies and letters to the emperors and senate, begging to be judged equally with the pagans. One such letter was Justin Martyr's, *First Apology* to the Emperor Antoninus Pius in which he presents the Christians' case.

By the mere application of a name, nothing is decided, either good or evil, apart from the actions implied in the name; and indeed, so far at least as one may judge from the name we are accused of, we are most excellent people... For from a name neither praise nor punishment could reasonably spring, unless something excellent or base in action be proved. And those among yourselves who are accused you do not punish before they are convicted; but in our case you receive the name as proof against us, and this although, so far as the name goes, you ought rather to punish our accusers. For we are accused of being Christians, and to hate what is excellent (Christian) is unjust.

... Wherefore we demand that the deeds of all those who are accused to you be judged, in order that each one who is convicted may be punished as an evil-doer, and not as a Christian; and if it is clear that any one is blameless, that he may be acquitted, since by the mere fact of his being a Christian he does no wrong.

And Tertullian, from his *Apology*, pleaded with the rulers of Rome:

If, again, it is certain that we are the most wicked of men, why do you treat us so differently from our fellows, that is, from other criminals, it being only fair that the same crime should get the same treatment? When the charges made against us are made against others, they are permitted to make use both of their own lips and of hired pleaders to show their innocence. They have full opportunity of answer and debate; in fact, it is against the law to condemn anybody undefended and unheard. Christians alone are forbidden to say anything in exculpation of themselves, in defense of the truth, to help the judge to a righteous decision; all that is cared about is having what the public hatred demands— the confession of the name, not examination of the charge: (*Apology*, Chap. 2.232).

Such was the generally held belief of the early Christians, a belief that cannot but be admired. Earlier, we quoted Tertullian as saying Christians would be perfectly suited for warfare except they counted it "better to be slain than to slay." Prior to Constantine's sanctioning of the Christian religion the Church was a spiritual entity; the first true Christians lived as they preached. But when Constantine invested the Church with power the persecuted began a slow evolution into becoming the persecutors. By the advent of Theodosius that slow evolution became a raging tide. Tertullian was writing about the year 200 CE; by the reign of Theodosius the Great (379 to 395) the Christians' sense of values had changed. No longer was there margin for differing beliefs—the Church reigned supreme. Theirs was the kingdom, and Theodosius was their civil arm.

As early as the middle of the second century, Irenaeus was already setting a goal that would see the Catholic Church "dispersed throughout the whole world, even to the ends of the earth." That was just what transpired during the period 100 to 500 CE. In exchange for Constantine's protection and religious freedoms, the Church worked frantically to bring about the unity of the people, and thereby, a strengthening of the empire. Where Jesus had resisted authoritative power, the Church sought it greedily. They designed an organization that was geared to manage large numbers of people. Spirituality was sacrificed for expediency. It didn't matter where one's heart was, only his loyalty. Anyone who confessed the creed and was baptized, obeyed the Church's hierarchy, and believed "the one and only truth from the Apostles, which is handed down by the Church" was a Christian. Rituals replaced the idea of Christian behavior.

⌐◅✾▻⌐

There are five kinds of synods according to their size: Diocesan, Provincial, National, Patriarchal and Ecumenical. Only the first three types convened before the third century. The Provincials were held in the cities once or twice a year under the supervision of the local bishop, whose intent was to gradually gain primacy over the other bishops of the province. It was in this same manner that the bishoprics in the larger cities such as Alexandria, Antioch and Rome began vying for dominance.

Until the entrance of Constantine and the Niecea Council (325 CE) the synodical meetings were public and the local populace had a voice in the proceedings. After the council of Nicea bishops alone were seated and the priests appeared thereafter merely as secretaries, or representatives of their bishops. The ecumenical council of Nice knew nothing of the five patriarchal cities; Alexandria, Rome, Antioch, Constantinople and Jerusalem that would later form the edifice of the Catholic hierarchy. Constantinople was yet to be built and Christianity was only taking root in Jerusalem. It would be decades before the friction between East and West split the Church into the Roman and Byzantine Empires.

The Church followed the lead of Constantine and the emperors who succeeded him during the period of the first seven ecumenical councils. (325-787 CE).

> The emperors after Constantine (as the popes after them) summoned the general councils, bore the necessary expenses, presided in the councils through commissions, gave to the decisions in doctrine and discipline the force of law for the whole Roman empire, and maintained them by their authority. The emperors nominated or confirmed the most influential metropolitans and patriarchs. They took part in all theological disputes, and thereby inflamed the passion of parties. They

protected orthodoxy and punished heresy with the arm of power. Often, however, they took the heretical side, and banished orthodox bishops from their sees. Thus Arianism, Nestorianism, Eutychianism, and Monophysitism successively found favor and protection at court (Philip Shaff, *History of the Christian Church*, vol. III, chap. 3).

It was only later, after the fall of the Roman Empire, that the Church attained the power to anoint emperors and dictate policies.

But what of the ecclesiastical dignitaries: the priests, bishops, and popes who formulated and sanctioned Church doctrines and regulations? How did they deport themselves in the assemblies? If a prerequisite for office was the possession of "charisma," and the "divine gift of grace," then one would suppose that, in emulation of their Master, the councils would be composed of quiet, peace-loving, intelligent men who were slow to anger, quick to pardon injuries, and impartial in judgment. When the councils were gathered, we might easily imagine refined gentlemen quietly and prayerfully discussing the issues before them. However, in reality, such was not the case. As we have already seen, there was contention on every level.

It might have been supposed that nowhere would Christianity appear in such commanding majesty as in a council, which should gather from all quarters of the world the most eminent prelates and the most distinguished clergy; that a lofty and serene piety would govern all their proceedings, and profound and dispassionate investigation exhaust every subject; that human passions and interest would stand rebuked before that awful assembly; that the sense of their own dignity as well as the desire of impressing their brethren with the solemnity and earnestness of their belief would at least exclude all intemperance of manner and language... History shows that melancholy reverse. Nowhere is Christianity less attractive, and if we look to the ordinary tone and character of the proceedings, less authoritative, than in the councils of the church. It is in general a fierce collision of two rival factions, neither of which will yield, each of which is solemnly pledged against conviction. Intrigue, injustice, violence, decisions on authority alone, and that the authority of a turbulent majority, decisions by wild acclamation rather then by sober inquiry, detract from the reverence, and impugn the judgments, at least of the later councils....rejoicing at the damnation imprecated against the humiliated adversary....the degeneracy is rapid from the council of Nicea to that of Ephesus, where each party came determined to use every means of haste, maneuver, court influence, bribery, to crush his adversary; where there was an encouragement of, if not an appeal to the violence of the populace, to anticipate the decrees of the council; where each had his own tumultuous foreign rabble to back his quarrel; and neither would scruple at any means to obtain the ratification of their anathemas through persecution by the evil government (H.H. Milman, D.D., *History of Latin Christianity*, New York, 1871, p 226).

Every congregation had its preferred books and every diocese its doctrines, especially later, between the Eastern and Western Churches. Even in the writings of Paul we read of open dissension within the Church. Heretical sects, such as the Gnostics, Arians, Eunomians, Semi-Arians, and Acacians, struggled constantly against, and often within, the orthodox Church. There was also a silent struggle between the Church and various Emperors—between the spiritual and the secular.

By the fourth century, Christians were willing to fight, rather than to die for their particular beliefs. By the fifth century, they had reverted back to the old Saul, "breathing out threatening and slaughter" against all dissenters. Such was the spirit that ruled most gatherings.

Together with abundant talents, attainments, and virtues, there were gathered also at the councils ignorance, intrigues, and partisan passions, which had already been excited on all sides by long controversies preceding and now met and arrayed themselves, as hostile armies, for open combat. For those great councils, all occasioned by controversies on the most important and the most difficult problems of theology, are, in fact, to the history of doctrine, what decisive battles are to the history of war. Just because religion is the deepest and holiest interest of man, are religious passions wont to be the most violent and bitter; especially in a time when all classes, from imperial court to market stall, take the liveliest interest in theological speculation, and are drawn into the common vortex of excitement. Hence the notorious rabies theologorum was more active in the fourth and fifth centuries than it has been in any other period of history... (Philip Shaff, *History of the Christian Church*, vol. III, chap. 5).

The brutality of the councils peaked at the synod that met in Ephesus in August of 449. Eutyches, the superior of a convent of monks, had been brought before the council to answer the charge of denying the two natures of Christ. The great Lutheran Church historian of the eighteenth century, Johann Lorenz von Mosheim, presents a very enlightening picture of the proceedings that followed.

> On the first mention of the two natures of Christ an angry dispute arose. But when the question put to Eutyches by Eusebius of Doryleum was read, whether he acknowledged the two natures after the incarnation, the assembly broke out with one voice, "Away with Eusebius! Banish Eusebius! Let him be burned alive! As he cuts asunder the two natures in Christ, so be he cut asunder!"... The Council proceeded to absolve Eutyches from all suspicion of heterodoxy, and to reinstate him in all his ecclesiastical honors; to depose Flavianus and Eusebius, and to deprive them of all their dignities. Flavianus alone pronounced his appeal; Hilarius, the Roman deacon, alone refused his assent. The unanimity of the assembly is unquestionable, but it is asserted, and on strong grounds, that it was an unanimity enforced by the dread of the imperial soldiery and the savage monks, who environed and even broke in, and violated the sanctity of the Council. ... Hilarius the deacon fled to Rome, but not so fortunate was Flavianus. After suffering personal insults, it is said even blows, from the furious Dioscorus himself, instigated by the monk Barsumas, who shouted aloud, "Strike him, strike him dead!" he expired after a few days, either of his wounds, of exhaustion, or mental suffering. Thus was this the first, but not the last Christian Council which was defiled with blood (Mosheim, *Eccl. Hist.*, Bk. 2, Cent. 5, pt. 2, ch. V, pp.288-289).

> At the third general council, at Ephesus, 431, all accounts agree that shameful intrigue, uncharitable lust of condemnation, and coarse violence of conduct were almost as prevalent as in the notorious robber-council of Ephesus in 449; though with the important difference, that the former synod was contending for truth, the latter for error. Even at Chalcedon, the introduction of the renowned expositor and historian Theodoret provoked a scene, which almost involuntarily reminds us of the modern brawls of Greek and Roman monks at the holy sepulcher under the restraining supervision of the Turkish police. His Egyptian opponents shouted with all their might: "The faith is gone! Away with him, this teacher of Nestorius!" His friends replied with equal violence: "They forced us [at the robber-council] by blows to subscribe; away with the Manichaeans, the enemies of Flavian,

the enemies of the faith! Away with the murderer Dioscorus? Who does not know his wicked deeds?" The Egyptian bishops cried again: "Away with the Jew, the adversary of God, and call him not bishop!" To which the oriental bishops answered: "Away with the rioters, away with the murderers! The orthodox man belongs to the council!" At last the imperial commissioners interfered, and put an end to what they justly called an unworthy and useless uproar (Philip Shaff, *History of the Christian Church*, vol. III, chap. 5).

St. Gregory Nazianzen, ... bishop of Constantinople, presided for a time over the second ecumenical council, had so bitter an observation and experience as even to lose, though without sufficient reason, all confidence in councils, and to call them in his poems "assemblies of cranes and geese." "To tell the truth ... I am inclined to shun every collection of bishops, because I have never yet seen that a synod came to a good end, or abated evils instead of increasing them. For in those assemblies (and I do not think I express myself too strongly here) indescribable contentiousness and ambition prevail, and it is easier for one to incur the reproach of wishing to set himself up as judge of the wickedness of others, than to attain any success in putting the wickedness away. Therefore I have withdrawn myself, and have found rest to my soul only in solitude." (Philip Shaff, *History of the Christian Church*, vol. III, chap. 5)

With these accounts the true picture and spirit of the Church is set forth, and yet, Dr. Shaff, ever the true believer, could still maintain, "In all these outbreaks of human passion, however, we must not forget that the Lord was sitting in the ship of the church, directing her safely through the billows and storms. The Spirit of truth, who was not to depart from her, always triumphed over error at last, and even glorified himself through the weaknesses of his instruments." I'm sure such reassurance would have provided comfort and succor to the countless millions of heretics who were brave enough to resist with their lives, or fearful enough to submit to Catholic suppression.

The canonization of the New Testament was a long process that began with Eusebius and continued for nearly a hundred years. As mentioned earlier, Eusebius divided the New Testament books into three classes, the "acknowledged," the "disputed," and the "heretical." He placed special emphasis on the four Gospels by calling them the "Holy Quaternion," and claiming we needed only four because of the four winds of the earth. The four Gospels along with Acts, thirteen epistles of Paul, I John, and I Peter were uncontested and constituted the "acknowledged" class. James, Jude, II Peter, and II and III John were placed in the "disputed" class, but were considered non-heretical. Also in the "disputed" class were books which Eusebius termed "base" or "counterfeit": the Acts of Paul, book of Hermas, Apocalypse of Peter, Epistle of Barnabas, Gospel of the Hebrews, a certain "Teachings of the Apostles", and, most confusingly, the Apocalypse of John which he also placed in the "acknowledged" category. As heretical forgeries he identified the Gospels of Peter, Thomas, and Matthias, and the Acts of Andrew, John, and others (*Ecclesiastical History*, 3.25.1-7 and 3.3.5-7).

Cyril, the Bishop of Jerusalem in about 356 CE and a member of the Eastern Church, came near to the final selection when he cataloged all the books in the present New Testament except Revelations, then added: "But let all the rest be excluded. And all the books which are not read in the churches, neither do thou read by thyself" (*Catech. Lect.*, iv. 35).

Finally, over three hundred years after the birth of Christianity it became apparent that the Fathers could not agree which books should be in the New Testament, and councils began to deal with the matter. The first synod to approach the subject was held in Laodicea in 365 CE. That meeting wasn't a general council, but its list was later adopted by the Church. It decreed that only canonical books of the Old and New Testament might be read, and listed the same books Cyril had chosen.

With only one book in question one would think that a solution was imminent, but we've already discovered the Church's penchant for division. Athanasius, Bishop of Alexandria, 365 CE, was at enmity with Eusebius and the clergy of Laodicea, and when Eusebius excluded Revelation, Athanasius immediately included it on his list. To further confuse the issue, he omitted Esther and inserted Baruch and the Letter of Jeremiah. Attempting to seal the issue, he ended by saying: "Let there be no mention of apocryphal writings."

At the same time, Amphilochius, the Bishop of Iconium, was preparing his New Testament. He accepted the four Gospels, Acts, and fourteen Epistles of Paul then added: "But some maintain that the Epistle to the Hebrews is spurious; not speaking well, for the grace is genuine. To proceed: What remains? Of the Catholic Epistles some maintain that we ought to receive seven, and others three only, one of James, and one of Peter, and one of John ... The Revelation of John again some reckon among (the scriptures); but still the majority say that it is spurious. This will be the most truthful canon of the inspired scriptures." From this we should be able to see that the issue was no where near a settlement.

About 389 CE, Gregory of Nezianzus gave as the New Testament: the four Gospels, Acts, fourteen Epistles of Paul, and the seven Catholic Epistles. He added, "In these you have all the inspired books; if there be any book besides these, it is not among the genuine (scriptures)" (Carm., xii. 31). The "seven Catholic Epistles" refer to James, I & II Peter, I, II & III John and Jude. Gregory was of the Eastern Church and also rejected Revelation.

In 390 CE, St. Augustine figured prominently in the establishment of the Bible. People attribute to God what was really the work of this one man. Augustine was the one who selected the books we now recognize as the New Testament. Although the councils decided upon the canon and their decisions were accepted by the entire Church, the decision was really that of Augustine, the leader of the council. The members gave very little study or research to the subject; indeed, how could they? There was no systematic study of paleography or archaeology. Any interest in past writings or cultures would have been more of a personal endeavor, and restricted to collecting folktales. Also, since the Church was more inclined to destroy books and records than preserve them, there would have been few available other than their own. Even more to the point, in a society where free thought could be hazardous to one's health, it was much safer to follow the Church's lead. At that time, Augustine was held in such high esteem they simply asked: "What did the early Fathers say?"

In relation to the New Testament, the synods which drew up lists of the sacred books show the opinion of some leading Fathers like Augustine, along with what custom had sanctioned. In this department no member of the synod exercised his critical faculty; a number together would decide such questions summarily. Bishops proceeded in the track of tradition or authority. Samuel Davidson, *The Canon of the Bible*, p. 172

In 393 CE, a council met in Hippo, Africa, to discuss the canon. They adopted St. Augustine's list in his presence; he was the ruling spirit.

The third council of Carthage was held in 397 CE. St. Augustine was again present. The council adopted this decree:

> It was also determined that besides the canonical scriptures, nothing be read in the church under the title of Divine scriptures. The Canonical scriptures are these:

Then follow the names of the books of the Bible as we have them now, with some variations in the order.

Although the Church leaders had made their decisions, not everyone accepted their choices. In the time of Didymus of Alexandria (392 CE), books that were not in the canon were read in the churches and were known to be spurious. And even though the canonical books were selected by the fifth century, St. Chrysostom, (approximately 407 CE), did not use II & III John, II Peter, Jude, and Revelation; all of which are in the Bible now. He also included the Wisdom of Jesus which, of course, isn't in the present Bible.

When Jerome composed his New Testament, in about 420 CE, he included Hebrews and Revelations, even though they were still frequently rejected. In another work, he included the Epistle of Barnabas in a canonical list and expressed doubts about Philemon, II Peter, Jude, and II & III John.

The *books* were finally selected, but the controversy continued into the sixteenth century, 1519, when Martin Luther disputed with Johann Eck at Leipzig. Luther denied papal authority and the canon of the Western Church by supporting the Hebrew Canon of the Eastern Church. The resulting split between Catholics and Protestants necessitated the Council of Trent in 1546, where the matter was settled—or was it?

> To meet this radical departure of the Protestants, and as well define clearly the inspired sources from which the Catholic Faith draws its defense, the Council of Trent among its first acts solemnly declared as "sacred and canonical" all the books of the Old and New Testaments "with all their parts, as they have been

used to be read in the churches, and as found in the ancient vulgate edition."

Still there must have remained some doubt because the Vatican Council of 1870 felt compelled to uphold the Council of Trent.

The Vatican Council took occasion of a recent error on inspiration to remove any lingering shadow of uncertainty on this head; it formally ratified the action of Trent and explicitly defined the Divine inspiration of all the books with their parts https://www.ecatholic2000.com/cathopedia/vol3/volthree245.shtml

So we see that even into the nineteenth century—eighteen hundred years after Christianity came upon the scene—the "divinely inspired" Word of God was still under dispute; selected or discarded by the debate of men. How then, can it be claimed the work of God?

The Christians' God is a fetish, an idol that men bow to when the heavens thunder confusion and fear. Faith is the blinders of reason, and reason is the bogeyman of ignorance.

THE TRUTH OF CHRISTIANITY

Do you ever notice how kids look up to their father, seeing him as the fountain of all wisdom and believing everything he says—until they near adulthood?

W hat are the claims on which Christianity bases its assertions? What evidence does it present to prove the validity of its God, that Jesus is his Son, or that Jesus died for the sins of the world? Where is the proof of all the stories in the New Testament? For that, we must turn to the Catholic Church, for it was that institution that chose the material and compiled the New Testament. Therefore it is to them we must turn for answers to our questions. From the Catholic Encyclopedia, concerning faith we find:

> "We believe", says the Vatican Council (III, iii), "that revelation is true, not indeed because the intrinsic truth of the mysteries is clearly seen by the natural light of reason, but because of the authority of God Who reveals them, for He can neither deceive nor be deceived." Thus, to return to the act of faith which we make in the Holy Trinity, we may formulate it in syllogistic fashion thus: Whatever God reveals is true but God has revealed the mystery of the Holy Trinity therefore this mystery is true. The major premise is indubitable and intrinsically evident to reason; the minor premise is also true because it is declared to us by the infallible Church, and also because, as the Vatican Council says, "in addition to the internal assistance of His Holy Spirit, it has pleased God to give us certain external proofs of His revelation, viz. certain Divine facts, especially miracles and prophecies, for since these latter clearly manifest God's omnipotence and infinite knowledge, they afford most certain proofs of His revelation and are suited to the capacity of all."
> https://www.ecatholic2000.com/cathopedia/indexf.shtml

First, we learn that revelations are true because God reveals them. Secondly, the "Holy Trinity" is true because God has revealed that mystery. Then we are assured that the major premise (that God reveals revelations) is "indubitable and intrinsically evident to reason". Let's pause here and consider these statements. Didn't we just read it was "... clearly seen by the natural light of reason ..." and can be "... indubitable and intrinsically evident to reason"? Why then, have debates and debacles been raging for nearly two thousand years? Why hasn't God done a better job revealing his marvelous truths?

And we're told "the minor premise" (God has revealed the Holy Trinity) is true because it is declared by the infallible Church. And further, the Vatican Council says that in addition to the Holy Spirit, God gave "certain external proofs of his revelation, viz. certain Divine facts, especially miracles and prophecies." And it is further stated that these miracles and prophecies clearly show God's omnipotence and infinite knowledge which prove his "revelation."

Now I'm going to be honest with you, I'm not a highly educated man, and when I run into phrases like, "major and minor premises" or "indubitable and intrinsically," I have to open up my dictionary and do some word study. And when I run that "indubitable and intrinsically" by old Webster I translate it into, "unquestionable and inherently evident to reason." Which sounds a lot like we're being told revelations should be believed simply for themselves, without any outside evidence. I do know I'm being told I should believe in the Holy Trinity because the "infallible Church" tells me it is true; and I should believe in a Divine God because the Vatican Council says his miracles and prophecies are Divine proofs.

First off, where is the proof God is Divine, or for that matter, that God even exists? Why should I accept that the Church is infallible, or that the miracles and prophecies are Divine proof? Where did all these suppositions come from? Just how did these ideas come into existence: that there is a God, that he is divine, that his revelations are true, that the Church is infallible, that Jesus is the son of God ... and so many, many more irrefutable facts? Let's stop and ask what we're being expected to believe on faith. First I'm expected to believe a person, minister or priest, perhaps someone I don't even know, who tells me fantastic stories of a Son of God, born of a virgin, who died for my sins, was resurrected and ascended to heaven. When I question his stories, I'm referred to a copy of a *sacred* book, written by fictitious authors, that no longer exist. When I question its authenticity, I'm assured that it was written by divinely inspired men and compiled by an infallible Church. And if I ask from where the Church received its authority I'm told it received a "supernatural prerogative … by a special Divine assistance." What does that mean? Did their God speak to them in a thundering decree, "YOU ARE INFALLIBLE!"? Or perhaps they bestowed that title upon themselves because they could kick every butt in the world? At any rate, these members of this infallible Church want me to take their word that their God bestowed upon them divine knowledge. And when I ask why I should believe in their God, do you know what I'm told? There is matter. You can't make something from nothing, so God had to make it. That's proof? Why a God? Why not a great explosion, an enormous energy force, an Ewack, or for that matter, how do they know it wasn't Zeus, or the Great Manitou?

The argument I'm trying to make is that at some point all these suppositions—and that is all they are—link to mortal, fallible man. For example, it is claimed God gave the Law to Moses; how do you know? Who said so? "The Law has been passed down to us." Says who? Again, I ask how do you know? The same argument can be made to refute the Gospels. How do you know who told them or who recorded them? How do we know Mary wasn't just a scared girl in trouble instead of a virgin? And the infallible Church! Really, isn't it obvious that Rome and the Catholic Church leaders got together and claimed infallibility simply to increase their power? When you strip away all the mystery and sanctity all you have is the Church saying Jesus is divine, Jesus saying God is divine and God saying the Church is infallible—each supporting the other and all drawn from a book written by dozens of unknown men over a period of 1800 years. In reality, we are not being asked to believe a supreme deity. At every point of contention, there stands a frail human being and that is where we are asked to place our trust.

But you insist, "The miracles and prophecies prove God's divinity!" Do they? Who recorded the miracles? Man. And what

prophecies have been fulfilled? The coming of the Son of God—
where is he? Who recorded those stories? Man. And if you'll study
Jesus' teachings you see he warned of a soon coming kingdom on
earth. That was two thousand years ago. What constitutes soon?

DISHARMONY OF THE GOSPELS

Prologue

For centuries, Christians have struggled to fit the jigsaw like pieces of the Gospels into one harmonious story of Jesus Christ and his ministry. Hundreds of thousands of books and articles have been published endeavoring to present a complete, harmonious picture. Most good Bibles even include a *Harmony of the Gospels* section in the appendix. Almost all churches have Bible studies that concentrate upon stubborn passages, and ministers devote entire sermons to hammering at odd shaped pieces. What is the end result? Ask any Christian and he'll open his Bible and assume a defensive crouch as he assures you that the Gospels do, indeed, harmonize—there are just some pieces that are "hard to understand." Others will claim there only appear to be contradictions because the authors have reported the story from different points of view. And a few might even admit to small, insignificant, translational errors.

One obstacle, the Gospel of John, is not so much a gaping hole as a stack of extra pieces, for while the other three Gospels appear to present a similar picture, John is nothing more than Church propaganda. Although it does refer to tales included in the other Gospels the writer's main intent was to establish the deity of Jesus. It wasn't written until at least 100 CE and wasn't accepted by the Church until the third century. For this reason, the theological world has separated Matthew, Mark, and Luke into what they refer to as the Synoptic Gospels. Some scholars will even admit that John doesn't harmonize.

Despite Christians' assertions that the Gospels present the same story, it simply isn't true. The only way one harmonious picture can be completed is by tossing the extra pieces aside and filling in the holes with faith. In others words, to paint the picture the Church presents of Jesus one must shift their brain into neutral and coast on faith. Yes, I know many Christians study the Scriptures diligently, but most study to confirm what they are taught each Sunday—not to discover truth. I know because I did so for nearly twenty years, and when I began to read with a critical eye it was amazing what I was able to discern.

Mark was the first gospel written, followed by Matthew, Luke, and much later, John. Only Luke was written by the author in the title. How can we be sure? There are a number of reasons, for instance: They were written late, at least thirty years after Jesus' death. All are translated from the Septuagint, the Greek version of scripture used by the Hellenistic Jews, rather than the Aramaic used by nationalistic Jews. And all were written for a gentile readership. One reason we know this is because Mark fails to mention a number of not only important but crucial events concerning Jesus—his miraculous birth, his genealogy, and childhood. Even the tale of his resurrection is an acknowledged late addition. This establishes it as the earliest gospel, and identifies all the added tales as just that—tales. For who would write a biography of George Washington and fail to mention he was President of the United States? Or, by the same token, exclude the information that the Son of God was born of a virgin? And how could a writer conclude such a story without including the miraculous resurrection at the ending?

Of the four Gospels, Matthew and Luke copied extensively from Mark. Matthew covers ninety percent of Mark. They have two hundred and fifty verses in common with many containing the same words and phrases. Matthew is the most Jewish of the Gospels, but as mentioned, quotes from the Septuagint. It doesn't explain Jewish customs and words, as Mark does, and in this sense seems to appeal to a more Jewish readership. The book wasn't completed until around 100CE.

There is another remarkable fact that raises a number of questions concerning the reliability of the Gospels. Although the Synoptic Gospels were written from late 1st century to early 2nd century, they're never quoted in later New Testament writings. Not even in the Acts of the Apostles, allegedly written by Luke. Here we have three works that copy freely, yet no one quotes them.

> When Hebrews talks of the "voice" of Christ today (1:2f, 2:11, 3:7, 10:5), why is it all from the Old Testament? When Paul, in Romans 8:26, says that "we do not know how we are to pray," does this mean he is unaware that Jesus taught the Lord's Prayer to his disciples? When the writer of 1 Peter urges, "do not repay wrong with wrong, but retaliate with blessing," has he forgotten Jesus' "turn the other cheek"? Romans 12 and 13 is a litany of Christian ethics, as is the Epistle of James and parts of the "Two Ways" instruction in the Didache and Epistle of Barnabas; but though many of these precepts correspond to Jesus' Gospel teachings, not a single glance is made in his direction. Such examples could be multiplied by the dozen.
>
> Earl Doherty - *The Jesus Puzzle*

Other than the Gospels, Ignatius, writing about 107 CE, is the first to mention such topics as Jesus' executioner, Pontius Pilate, and Mary, Jesus' mother. The earliest reference to Jesus as any kind of a teacher comes in 1 Clement shortly afterward. To find the first indication of Jesus as a miracle worker, we must move beyond Ignatius to the Epistle of Barnabas. Imagine, the Gospels were compiled from oral tradition decades after Jesus' death—people were talking of the events—yet no one else was inclined to record those events. Why?

By 130 CE, the canonical books of the New Testament were written, without benefit of the Gospels. But what of the oral tales, why were they not noted and included in other writings? Perhaps they were only relevant to a small, local sect. For whatever reason, the gospel tales of Jesus had little appeal until the third century.

But for our study, let's start with Luke's story since it has the earliest chronological beginning.

Disharmony of the Gospels

Luke, Chapter 1 & 2

The writer of Luke, addressing a Theophilus, affirms there were "many" who recorded the stories of the Christian beliefs—

two were surely Mark and Matthew. He also tells his readers he "had perfect understanding of all things from the very first" then, immediately launches into a series of fantastic tales: The miraculous conceptions of Jesus, and John the Baptist. A prophecy of Jesus as the Son of God. The story of the census and a trip to Bethlehem. An expanded nativity narrative with the appearance of angels. The confirmation of Jesus as the Christ by Simeon and Anna. And finally, the child Jesus astounding the doctors. All these wonderful and fascinating stories of Jesus' early life, never before recorded, suddenly revealed by Luke—decades after their alleged occurrences. Stories, which Mark or Matthew apparently didn't think important enough to mention—or had never heard. But are they true? Of course not. We know they're spurious because the concept of Jesus as the Son of God was not widely accepted until after the destruction of Jerusalem in 70 CE. The idea of Jesus as the Son of God was a Hellenistic concept the Apostles and true followers of Jesus never recognized. With the exception of Paul's writings all the books in the New Testament WERE WRITTEN BY GENTILES OR HELLENISTIC JEWS!

After the Jewish War, the Jews were hated and labeled as Christ-killers. Over a million were slaughtered in the war and nearly one hundred thousand enslaved. For a Jew to enter a Christian congregation would have been suicide. For further proof, see Acts 21:20-26 where thousands of believing Jews were still keeping the Law and worshiping in the temple. If Jesus' Apostles had proclaimed him the Son of God, the orthodox Jews would have stoned them as they did Stephen. For this fact alone, any references inferring the Apostles viewed Jesus as the Son of God can only be a figure of speech such as many Christians use today when they refer to one another as a "child of God" or "son of God." Otherwise, such passages have to be later interpolations (See Matthew 14:33 & 16:16).

And there is an even simpler reason that marks them false. Popular myths tend to grow, not shrink. Unimportant events might be dropped or omitted from tales, but never the exciting, sensational, and more informative parts. Considering Mark, and Matthew's propensity to copy, had they known of the events Luke recorded they most certainly would have been included in their works. Also the author of Luke practically told us his intention when he stated that "eyewitnesses" had already told the stories, but he was going to give

Theophilus something that would make it more certain. What? What was different about his gospel? New stories. Where did they come from? Had the author of Luke been secretly harboring unknown tales of Jesus? Or did he just invent some? Today falsification of stories or events is considered lying and in some cases is illegal, but such was not the case when the New Testament books were being written. Students often viewed their ideas and deductions as extensions of their master and believed what they spoke—or wrote—was actually the values of their teacher. Adding to another writer's work or even signing a prominent author's name to one's own writings was a common practice.

The events depicting the life of Jesus in the Gospels are fabricated history, written years after Christianity came upon the scene. Written expressly to fortify and strengthen a doctrinal position, or fulfill a fancied prophecy. As we have seen, the Jesus birth story in Luke is a prime example: in it we find a passage written to establish the preeminence of Jesus' ministry over that of John (1:5-17, 41-45), another to introduce the Immaculate Conception and virgin birth (1:26-35), one which identifies Jesus as the Son of God (1:35); the Davidic line of birth is proclaimed (1:27, 32, & 2:4), it establishes Bethlehem as the birthplace that one prophecy might be fulfilled (2:4-7), and a return to Nazareth to fulfill the requirement that he be a Nazarene (2:39). Jesus' divinity is reinforced by the declarations of Simeon & Anna, (2:25-38). Jesus is shown confounding the doctors in the Jerusalem temple to display his supernatural abilities, (2:41-47). Lastly, there is the cryptic verse in which Jesus practically admits his divinity (2:49).

All these items garnered from only two chapters—truly a comprehensive endeavor. Someone really had to work to package and market all that without the benefits of our electronic age. Of course, he had a lot of help since the virgin birth story is on the order of mythic fiction, and the incident of Jesus confounding the doctors is plagiarized from the autobiography of Josephus, the noted Jewish historian. The Bethlehem birth, which makes Jesus of the family of David, is founded on nothing but arbitrary interpretation of prophecy and is full of contradictions. For while Luke has his characters living in Nazareth and places the birth in Bethlehem, Matthew identifies Bethlehem as their home city and stages a flight into Egypt with a return to Nazareth to fulfill prophecy. Further, it's unclear why Joseph, as a descendant of David, should have to report to a place that was vacated by his ancestors a thousand years earlier. This public relations guru also goofed by dating the birth of Jesus during the reign of Herod—who died in 4 CE—and in the year of the census that took place after the deposition of Herod's son, Archilaus, ten years later.

Matthew Chapter 1 & Luke 3

MATTHEW BEGINS with the genealogy of Jesus, in an attempt to establish Joseph as his father, while Luke inserts his genealogy in the third chapter, after Jesus is baptized by John. Here we find an enormous conflict because while both lines allegedly trace the lineage of Joseph, they are different. Joseph doesn't even have the same father or grandfather! Now I've heard a number of different excuses that attempt to explain the contradictions: The Jews reckon descent differently. Not all descendants were included. Luke added extra names to have a major character appear on the scene every seven years. Or one line of descent is related to Mary. The simplest reason I can think of is that the writers simply didn't agree. However, it really isn't important, because both uphold Joseph as Jesus' father and therefore make the virgin birth story simply a folktale. In Luke 3:23, in referring to Joseph as Jesus' father the author, or someone, tried to correct the oversight by slipping in the phrase "as was supposed" to cast doubt upon Joseph's paternity. But Paul, writing about twenty years before Mark, makes no reference to a virgin birth. He stated Jesus was made of a woman (Galatians 4:4) and of the seed of David (Romans 1:3). The virgin birth isn't mentioned in Revelations or any of the epistles. In fact, it spoils attempts to trace Jesus' lineage to the Davidic line by making him divine through a virgin birth. In Luke 2:22-38 Mary and Joseph are described as his parents when they go to the temple for Mary's purification ritual—a tale obviously concocted before the invention of the virgin birth story. And why should we give credence to such a story? Where did it originate? How do we know Mary and Joseph's story is true? We cannot suppose that a physical examination established her virginity, because it took the assurance of an angel to convince Joseph. And why should we believe an angel spoke to them? What validation do we have? None. Only the word of an unknown author who said Mary said thus and so. If a pregnant teenager today claimed she had been impregnated by a spirit would we believe her? Of course not! Who would be so gullible? Why then should we be expected to believe some unknown, unidentifiable, writer who lived two thousand years ago?

Matthew Chapter 2

From the first sentence we're bombarded with questions. Immediately, I wonder what Mary and Joseph were doing in Bethlehem. Did they live there or, as Luke tells us, were they there to report for a census? Luke goes into great detail concerning the genealogy and birth of Jesus while Matthew concentrates on events after the birth, that is, Herod's alleged massacre of the infants, and Mary and Joseph's flight into Egypt. We might assume that Luke, writing after Matthew, just didn't wish to repeat stories already told. However, if that were the case he would have known of the flight to Egypt tale and would not have contradicted it with the casual mention of a peaceful return to Nazareth (Luke 2:39).

My Thompson Chain Reference Bible identifies the keyword of Matthew as "fulfilled" and the "Emphatic Thought" as, "Fulfillment of Old Testament Prophecy." So intent was the writer on fulfilling those prophecies that he wasn't above inventing stories, as is the case with Herod's slaughter of the male infants. It is easy to see that another purpose was to establish doctrinal dominance. "Fulfilled" might also apply to the writer's efforts to anticipate and answer every doctrinal question that ever arose, or might ever arise. He is reaching, straining, grasping with every syllable to show Jesus as the fulfillment of every messianic prophecy he can conjure up from the Hebrew Scriptures.

Almost from the beginning he tries to establish Jesus' divinity. In 1:23 we read:

> Behold a virgin shall be with child, and shall bring forth a son, and they shall call his name Emmanuel, which being interpreted is, God with us.

This is the pivotal scripture used to prove the miraculous virgin birth of the Son of God, it along endorses the deity of Jesus—and it falls flat. The passage is an almost direct quotation of Isaiah 7:14, where it is a sign to King Ahab, and had nothing whatsoever to do with Jesus' conception or birth. The Hebrew word for virgin used in Isaiah, *almah*, means a young woman—today we might say teenager—which may or may not have had prior sexual experience. It does not mandate she be a virgin. Anytime the Bible wants to make a distinction between a virgin and non-virgin for legal reasons—as in a court of Law in matters of divorce—the term *betulah*—virgin— is used and never *almah*.

Isaiah tells Ahab that a young woman, with prior sexual experience since he used *almah*, shall conceive and bear a child, and before that child (verse 16) shall know to refuse the evil and choose the good, the land that he feared—Assyrian invaders—will be forsaken by both her kings. A child learns right from wrong usually by the age of 2-3 years. If you keep reading the passage you will find that within about 2-3 years—before the child learns good from bad—God would bring His Presence, Immanuel, (God with Israel), upon Israel and destroy the attacking Assyrian army. The young woman's pregnancy was a sign that something *good* was going to happen to Israel—within the near future. The child was a sign of the soon coming delivering Presence of God as he liberated his people from Assyrian aggression. God's Presence—not Jesus'—would come and destroy Israel's enemy. The child was not to destroy them—God was to destroy them. Thus we see that to adhere to a virgin birth, in front of such solid evidence is foolishness, and to believe that this child is Jesus is ridiculous, because Jesus would not be born for seven hundred more years.

Matthew is anxious to show Jesus as the fulfillment of Old Testament prophecy. His approach is to interpret current events as prophesied by the Scriptures. His method is one used by the Qumran community—the Essenes of the Dead Sea Scrolls—termed the *pesher*. He records five scriptural references in the birth narrative to show that prophecy was fulfilled in Jesus. And his quotations are seldom precise. He did just what the sectarians of Qumran did— changed the quotations just enough to suit his purpose.

He also used another type of rabbinic biblical interpretation known as *midrash*—referring to multiple scriptures—and employed a principle called *gezerah shawah*, which we mentioned earlier. This was a common practice, used repeatedly by New Testament writers.

Regarding the story of Herod's slaughter of the infants, both Luke and Matthew state that Herod was the ruler at the time of Jesus' birth. And, as already mentioned, Luke further enlightens us with the census taking ordered by Emperor Augustus at the time that Quirinius (Cyrenius) was Roman governor of Syria. The only problem is that Herod was dead long before Quirinius ruled Syria. This conflict either puts the lie to Luke's tale, Matthew's story of Herod's atrocities, or both.

Mark Chapter 1, Matthew Chapter 3, Luke Chapter 3

As stated earlier, Mark was the first of the Gospels written. The book opens with the baptism of Jesus at the beginning of his ministry and makes no mention of his birth, childhood, or early life. This is the first incident covered by all four Gospels. Unlike the previous events we've just discussed in Matthew and Luke, this story is quite possibly based on more than a zealous writer's imagination. However, it has been Hellenized to the point where the original Judaic interpretations are barely discernible. All three Gospels have been written or rewritten to exalt Jesus as the Son of God—not the Messiah. Old Testament prophecies are taken out of context in an effort to show Jesus as their fulfillment. The language is Hellenistic Christian in that the mindset is of Jesus as the Son of God who comes with judgment and the out-pouring of the Holy Ghost. To see through all the window dressing we must remember a couple of facts: First, the Jews were looking for a messiah in the mold of David, a warrior who would drive the Romans from the land and usher in the Kingdom of God on earth. The idea of a Son of God incarnate in a man who taught escape to an inner spiritual kingdom was not only unheard of, it was unacceptable to the Jews, then as it is today. Any Jew attempting such a role would have been stoned—it was blasphemy to equate one's self with God. Secondly, both John and Jesus came preaching repentance for entrance into the coming Kingdom of God—not the Hellenistic Gospel of Christ. Any statement that contradicts these facts should be regarded as false. When Jesus began preaching, he didn't bring a new message, his was the same as John the Baptist's:

> Now after John was handed over, Jesus came into Galilee, preaching the gospel of the kingdom of God, and saying, "The time is fulfilled, and the kingdom of God is at hand: repent ye, and believe the gospel" ['good news'--not the Gospels] (Mk. 1:14&15).

When he said, "The time is fulfilled ..." he was implying that whoever was judging time had reason to believe that something important was about to happen. The Essenes, the writers of the Dead Sea Scrolls, were the ones studying times, watching current events, and trying to foresee God's intentions. What was Jesus' message? The kingdom is coming. The kingdom is near, doesn't sound very imperative to us. After all, Christians have been waiting two thousand years for that promise. But to the Jews, who were living for and expecting God's retribution upon the Romans, it was a call to arms. This was Jesus' message, this is what he taught, not some form of spiritual escapism. Jesus was preaching the coming kingdom in a matter that set him apart from the other insurrectionist who had marched against Jerusalem in armed rebellion. According to the Essenes, an army without the backing of a repentant Israel could not oust the Romans. But a repentant Israel would bring God's holy army, and God would overthrow the wicked. That was Jesus' message, "Repent, the kingdom of God is at hand."

The first three verses of Mark immediately identify it as Hellenistic, since it refers to the gospel of Jesus Christ instead of the gospel of the Kingdom, which Jesus preached. Also, Jesus is quickly identified as the Son of God, a Hellenistic concept that developed early in the second century and was made concrete in the fourth when Constantine proclaimed Jesus of the same substance as God. In these verses, we also have one of the first of many hybrid prophecies. Here two prophecies have been combined to try and make them identify John the Baptist as the forerunner of Jesus. Because, even after John's death, he still had his own followers who believed he was the promised messiah. The whole scenario of John baptizing Jesus was written, along with a number of other incidents, to show John as subservient to Jesus. The prophecies referred to are in Isaiah 40:3 and Malachi 3:1, but they are not speaking of John nor the Son of God. Both are judgment prophecies referring to the coming of God and the establishment of his kingdom on earth. In the quote from Malachi there has been a subtle change.

> Behold, I will send my messenger, and he shall prepare the way before me: and the Lord, whom ye seek, shall suddenly come to his temple, even the messenger of the covenant, whom ye delight in: behold, he shall come, saith the LORD of hosts (Mal. 3:1).

The writer of Mark wants the messenger to precede the messiah—Jesus:

> As it is written in the prophets, Behold, I send my messenger before thy face, which shall prepare thy way before thee (Mk. 1:2).

So he writes "before thy face" but in Malachi God wanted the messenger to appear before his (God's) face. The "messenger" was the expected messiah, not a forerunner to Jesus, and it was God who was to come with judgment upon Israel, not a redeemer. Careful reading of Malachi 3 with the last sentence of chapter 2 reveals that the messenger is the long awaited messiah, the one to come is God, and the event is the Day of Judgment.

And we find another twist of words in the statement:

> The voice of one crying in the wilderness, Prepare ye the way of the Lord, make his paths straight. John did baptize in the wilderness, and preach the baptism of repentance for the remission of sins (Mk. 1:3-4).

The Gospels pretend that the Mosaic Law has been revoked by Jesus, so the writer here tries to present salvation through Jesus when the original is speaking of the spreading of the Law.

> The voice of him that crieth in the wilderness, Prepare ye the way of the Lord, make straight in the desert a highway for our God (Is. 40:3).

In the *Community Rule*, from the Dead Sea Scrolls, the Essenes quoted this passage when referring to themselves:

> ...they shall be separated from the midst of the gatherings of the men of wrongs to go to the wilderness to prepare there the way of the Lord, as it is written: "In the wilderness prepare the way of the Lord: make straight in the desert a highway for God." **[And they unmistakably identify the highway as the Law.]** This is the study of the Law, as he commanded them through Moses to do all that has been revealed from age to age, and, by his holy spirit, as the prophets revealed.

The "wilderness" spoken of in verse 3 does not refer to John's physical environment. In Isaiah it is a metaphor likening a chastised and beaten Jerusalem—Israel—to a landscape: The people are grass (see Isaiah 40:6&7). The valleys are the poor and oppressed. The mountains are the rich and powerful, etc. The crier is, again, the messenger expounding the Law, warning of the coming of God and the Day of Judgment. Verse 5 states that "all flesh," meaning all people, shall see the glory of the Lord "together." This cannot be a reference to Jesus because only a few people saw him and the reign of God on earth has yet to occur (See Isaiah 40: 9-11).

Truly both John and Jesus did preach repentance and baptism, but as a Jewish purification ritual. Such a rite was special to the Jews and was often used by soldiers before going into battle. It was an oath of allegiance and a holy sacrament. The Essenes' *Community Rule* prescribed washing in water for those who had repented. Here also, is a logical explanation as to why the "Son of God" was in need of baptism. Everyone who transgressed God's word was unclean and everyone, all Israel, had transgressed by allowing the foreigners to rule. Even a potential messiah, to the Jews a man with supernatural powers, had to be washed clean of sin by baptism.

Look at how expanded additions have exploited the events. In Mark's accounts of Jesus' baptism we have a short, concise tale. Jesus came to John, was baptized, the Holy Spirit descended upon him in the form of a dove and a voice from heaven proclaimed, "Thou art my beloved Son, in whom I am well pleased." Luke tells a like story, but Matthew includes the additional information that John recognized Jesus and protested his unworthiness whereupon Jesus reassured him. And the Gospel of John, if you can put any faith in it, has John announcing the "Lamb of God, which taken away the sins of the world" before Jesus even arrives on the scene. According to this Gospel, John had already been proclaiming Jesus as his replacement. However, according to John 1:33, he didn't know Jesus. He only knew that the redeemer would be revealed to him, because that was the reason he had been called to baptize. God—the one who sent him to baptize—told him, "Upon whom thou shalt see the Spirit descending, and remaining on him, the same is he which baptizeth with the Holy Ghost." John stated that he saw those things and bare record that Jesus was the Son of God.

Now, let's look at Matthew 11:2-6 & Luke 7:18-23, John is in prison and sends two of his disciples to reaffirm Jesus' identity. Why? Allegedly, John baptized him, touched him, saw the fulfillment of a commandment that placed him in the position of a prophet, saw the Holy Ghost descending upon Jesus, and actually heard the voice of God proclaiming his Son. What more powerful assurance could his disciples possibly bring him? None—all references to the event were written or rewritten specifically to depict John as subservient to Jesus. Other points to consider: According to Luke 1:36-41, the mothers of Jesus and John were cousins who knew and visited one another. Both knew their pregnancies were divine. Both knew the roles their children were to play, and John even recognized Jesus in the womb. Does it seem likely that the two children would grow up without John knowing that Jesus was the Son of God—the one he was to baptize?

Under careful examination, the truth of this passage becomes apparent. Both John and Jesus preached the same message: repent for the kingdom of heaven is at hand (Matthew 3:2, 4:23 & Mark 1:15). Notice, this was not a new message. It was not the introduction of an indwelling kingdom. This was the same message the Jews had dreamed of and looked forward to for hundreds of years—the promise of God's kingdom upon earth. Look closely, John does not mean Jesus when he speaks of someone coming whose shoes he's not worthy to unloose (Mark 1:7). If this was originally a true story of Jesus' ministry, then we have already established the purpose of that ministry—the messenger was to be a leader molded after the great prophets of ancient Israel. The message was the coming of the Kingdom of God and freedom from oppression. This is what the prophecies in Malachi and Isaiah promised and it's what John described. Look at Matthew 3:9-12. Who is able to raise up children unto Abraham—God or Jesus? Who was to bring judgment and cast those found lacking into a fire—God or Jesus? Who was the giver of the Holy Spirit (Ezekiel 36:27, Zechariah 12:10, & Numbers 11:25)? Who was to judge the world? Here, as in Mark and Luke, Christianity has transformed the story of Jesus, the expected deliver of Israel, into an avenging/loving Son of God. Ask yourself, does the Messiah Jesus fit the role of a judgmental god who was to fulfill metaphors such as "chopping down" the wicked and casting them into the fire, or "purging the threshing floor"—again the wicked— with unquenchable fire? If so, at what point in his ministry did it occur? Look at Luke 3:15-17, the people were wondering if John was the messiah. Did John deny it? No, he delivered his message just as a capable messenger should. And what was that message? God was coming in judgment—not Jesus. The conclusion should be obvious. What we have is a Hebrew story corrupted with Christian fables.

Mark 1:14-6:6, Matthew 4:12-13:58 & Luke 4:14-30

In Mark we have the introduction of Jesus' early ministry:

Now after that John was put in prison, Jesus came into Galilee, preaching the gospel of the kingdom of God, saying, "The time is fulfilled, and the kingdom of God is at hand: repent ye, and believe the gospel." (Mk. 1-14)

Really, hardly more than a simple admonition, but Matthew saw the opportunity to throw in another fulfilled prophecy.

Now when Jesus had heard that John was cast into prison, he departed into Galilee; And leaving Nazareth, he came and dwelt in Capernaum, which is upon the sea coast, in the borders of Zabulon and Nephthalim: That it might be fulfilled which was spoken by Esaias the prophet, saying, "The land of Zabulon, and the land of Nephthalim, by the way of the sea, beyond Jordan, Galilee of the Gentiles; The people which sat in darkness saw

great light; and to them which sat in the region and shadow of
death light sprung up." From that time Jesus began to preach,
and say, "Repent: for the kingdom of heaven is at hand." (Matt.
4:12-17)

There is no such prophecy recorded by Esaias or anywhere in
the Old Testament. The only place it is found is in the gospel of
Matthew. Esaias does speak of the Gentiles coming to the light, but
passages such as Isaiah 50:10-11, 51:4-7, and 60:1-5 make it obvious
that "light" meant an understanding of God's Law—not Jesus Christ.

In this passage Matthew has Jesus going to Capernaum and then
back to Nazareth before he begins calling his disciples, an incident
Mark omitted (See Matthew 4:18 & Mark 1:14-16). Since the author
didn't quote from Isaiah, just where did he get his information? Was
it a miraculous revelation from God? Was he privy to information
unknown to Mark? Or, perhaps he simply saw an opportunity to slip
in another *prophecy* in order to lend credence to the idea of Jesus'
divinity. Note how the prophetic reference is inserted neatly between
the two verses from Mark, copied almost word for word. But it is
in Luke where we find an inspired writer. He provides so much
additional information we can't help but wonder where it originated,
since Mark and Matthew fail to mention it.

And Jesus returned in the power of the Spirit into Galilee: and
there went out a fame of him through all the region round about.
And he taught in their synagogues, being glorified of all. And he
came to Nazareth, where he had been brought up: and, as his
custom was, he went into the synagogue on the Sabbath day,
and stood up for to read. And there was delivered unto him the
book of the prophet Esaias. And when he had opened the book,
he found the place where it was written, "The Spirit of the Lord is
upon me, because he hath anointed me to preach the gospel to
the poor; he hath sent me to heal the brokenhearted, to preach
deliverance to the captives, and recovering of sight to the blind,
to set at liberty them that are bruised, To preach the acceptable
year of the Lord." And he closed the book, and he gave it again
to the minister, and sat down. And the eyes of all them that were
in the synagogue were fastened on him. And he began to say
unto them, "This day is this scripture fulfilled in your ears." And
all bare him witness, and wondered at the gracious words which
proceeded out of his mouth. And they said, "Is not this Joseph's
son?" And he said unto them, "Ye will surely say unto me this

proverb, Physician, heal thyself: whatsoever we have heard done in Capernaum, do also here in thy country." And he said, "Verily I say unto you, No prophet is accepted in his own country. But I tell you of a truth, many widows were in Israel in the days of Elias, when the heaven was shut up three years and six months, when great famine was throughout all the land; But unto none of them was Elias sent, save unto Sarepta, a city of Sidon, unto a Woman that was a widow. And many leper were in Israel in the time of Eliseus the prophet; and none of them was cleansed, saving Naaman the Syrian." And all they in the synagogue, when they heard these things, were filled with wrath, and rose up, and thrust him out of the city, and led him unto the brow of the hill whereon their city was built, that they might cast him down headlong. But he passing through the midst of them went his way (Lu. 4:14-30).

Please notice that Luke didn't use Matthew's Isaiah quote; instead he turned to another Isaiah scripture. Is it possible he knew Matthew's passage was an interpolation?

One type of error commonly committed in Bible interpretation is when intelligent and learned men, attempting to psychoanalyze a passage, take it out of context to support their supposition. A good example may be found in a commentary by a noted theologian; I'll not identify the writer for obvious reason. In referring to Jesus' rejection in his home town, Nazareth, as recorded in the above passage. The noted professor disagreed with the more conventional interpretation that the people became angry with Jesus because he made the presumptuous claim that he was the messenger referenced by the prophet Esaias. The professor contented that the people were angry because Jesus offended their sensibilities by saying God was interested in people other than Jews when he referred to the non-Jewish widow in Sarepta, and Naaman, the Syrian.

He built on this passage, and took special note of Jesus' youth and presumed inexperience, the peoples' recognition of his linage, and their attempt to cast him from a cliff. He presented a great argument, but fail to check the foundation.

When one studies the occasion of Jesus' homecoming as recorded in Mark and Matthew, and compares the incidents preceding and following the event, some startling differences become evident.

All three accounts record Satan's temptation of Jesus in the wilderness and Jesus' journey to Galilee, prior to his return to

Nazareth. In Luke, the mission to Galilee is summed up in two verses: Jesus went to Galilee, became famous, taught in their synagogues, and went to Nazareth. However, Luke, as noted above, has much to say concerning Jesus' homecoming. He mentions the name of the city along with the information that it was where Jesus was reared. It also states that he went into the synagogue, as was his custom, and stood up to read. The book of Esaias was given to him and he read the first verse of chapter sixty-one and the first part of the second verse—stopping short of proclaiming God's day of vengeance.

The account goes into great detail, even stating that he closed the book, handed it to the minister, and sat down. Then, with all eyes upon him, he stated, "This day is this scripture fulfilled in your ears." Notice the tension built by the writer. It's almost like a screenplay.

Then the people bare him witness, wondered at his words, and acknowledged him as the son of Joseph. There is no inference of anger. This was one reason the professor rejected the notion that the people became angry because of his presuming to be the messenger of the Isaiah scripture. They become angry after his next speech in which he lauds the Gentiles over the Jews. It was at this point the crowd rose up and carried him out of the city and attempted to toss him over a cliff.

Using only this passage the professors' interpretation appears to be correct. But let's walk around this vehicle and kick all the tires.

In the Mark version, we learn that the two Luke verses covering Jesus' sojourn in Galilee has been expanded to over four and a half chapters in Mark which goes into great detail about Jesus' ministry in that country and the message he preached—repentance and the coming kingdom of God. He called his disciples, worked miracles and disputed with the Pharisees and scribes. It isn't until the sixth chapter that Jesus returns to Nazareth. Only the incident is so insignificant that the city isn't even mentioned, it's only stated that he "… came into his own country." The entire Nazareth incident is covered in six verses. He preached in the synagogue and astounded everyone with his wisdom. He was acknowledged as the son of Mary, and the people were offended by this realization. Notice that here it is stated emphatically why the people were offended. Jesus then made the famous remark that a prophet is without honor in his own country. He could do no mighty works, so he healed a few sick people and left, marveling because of their unbelief.

Here we have an entirely different picture. There's no reference to, or quotation from the book of Esaias. And notice the conflict with the professor's position. The main passage upon which he builds his argument, the one in which Jesus praises the Gentiles, isn't even mentioned.

In Matthew we find similar occurrences: Jesus went to Galilee after hearing that John had been cast into prison, preached repentance and the coming kingdom of God, and delivered his Sermon on the Mount—which covers three chapters. He worked miracles and cast out demons. Then, in chapter 13, he "came into his own country" and again, there's no mention of the name of the city, which may be significant in more than one way because there are no records that Nazareth even existed at that time. This account is truly interesting. There is hardly anything mentioned within it that relates to the other two tales: no Isaias, no prophecy fulfillment, no raging mob—nothing. Jesus isn't even acknowledged as a citizen of that city. The error that the professor made is a common one among those who never question the validity of their study material. They get so focused on developing a premise until they fail to see they're nit-picking a folktale or a counterfeit passage.

In defense, you might point out that many events were often omitted from one gospel or another, but it should be recognized that many events were added to all the Gospels. Here, we have a prime example. Notice the context and what was happening. The writer of Luke's main agenda was to Christianize Jesus. As I mentioned earlier, Jesus and his Apostles were Jews and observed the Law. Anywhere you find them behaving contrary to that Law you can rest assured that it is a forged or altered passage.

Here the writer of Luke depicts Jesus as a rising star much in demand in the synagogues. And while there's nothing unusual about three people describing the same event from different perspectives I see the trend referred to in my earlier commentary on Luke, whereby tales tend to grow with age, repeated again and again throughout the Gospels. And they are added with such tactless regularity as to resemble a Church shopping list of doctrinal issues in need of Jesus' endorsement. Almost all the additions are introduced to strengthen or enforce a controversial Church issue, or promote the supernatural power of Jesus.

The next few chapters of all three synoptic gospels record short, exaggerated, incidents of Jesus' ministry: healings, the casting out of demons, and discourses on various topics. The stories give every indication of someone recording condensed versions of oral traditions. To illustrate, I have never read the journals of Lewis and Clark, but I have heard stories and read references of their travels. Today I could take a copy of those journals and record precise accounts of what happened, when and where, on specific dates. And in many cases I could even accurately convey the author's reasoning and thoughts. However, if I had to rely on my own knowledge I could only relate vague tales.

Even though I've seen pictures of Lewis and Clark I could only describe them as one having dark hair the other being redheaded. I have no idea of the Indian maiden's appearance, what she wore or her physical stature. I can't even spell or pronounce her name. Obviously, the writers of the Gospels had the same problems. We have only a vague description of Jesus' appearance, and none of the disciples are described. There are hardly any references to any daily activities that might give us insight into the character and lives of these founders of a new religion. Why? Was it because the writers simply felt it unimportant, or because those memories were lost with the passing of time? The fact that the writers following Mark include additional miracles and tales indicate that perhaps the stories only came into being with the passage of time. And the blatant fabrications of John make it certain.

It is surmised that John was written early in the second century, but most likely much later, about one hundred years after the incidents it records. At that time, the divinity of Jesus was one of the most contented issues among the many Christian sects. And that one topic introduced countless other questions: If he was God, when did he become God? Was he God from birth, if so, how could he also be a man? These and numerous other questions split the Christian world into camps that often resorted to physical combat. The Book of John was written explicitly to substantiate the deity of Jesus.

Mark 3:13-19, Matthew 10:1-42 & Luke 6:12-16

The events described in these passages tell us Jesus selected his twelve Apostles and sent them to preach, to heal the sick, and cast out demons. At least that is the statement we find in Mark and

Luke. However, Matthew, always the opportunist, saw a chance to insert a sermon by Jesus. He practically quotes the passage from Mark then launches into detailed instructions for the Apostles' commission: where they were to go, what they were to carry, and who they were to see. Then he launches into dire warnings of the end time judgment and the persecutions of not just the Apostles, but all believers. In the end, he extends vague, undefined rewards for the faithful. The entire passage appears to be nothing more than a tirade of prevailing beliefs.

Just a cursory glance might lead one to think the writer simply inserted his own sermon and attributed it to Jesus, as was the common practice of the early Church writers, but closer scrutiny reveals a number of statements that indicate an oral Judaic tradition. The first is in verse five through seven where the twelve are to go only to "the lost sheep of the house of Israel," and preach the gospel of the kingdom. The second is a reference in verse 18 where Jesus said the Apostles would be witnesses against the Gentiles. Then in 34, Jesus warns of violence and unrest. These were Jewish ideas taught by Jesus. The first two teach explicitly that the message of the kingdom was only for the Jews. This is also substantiated in Matthew 15:21-24 where Jesus declared his ministry was only for Israel, and referred to the Gentiles as "dogs"—abominable, unclean, flesh eaters. These teachings put the lie to the *great commission*, found in Matthew 28:18-20, because Jesus never taught of an indwelling, spiritual kingdom available to all. Throughout his entire ministry, even in the end, Jesus expected a literal, earthly kingdom led by a revitalized Israel. It is what he taught and also what his disciples believed and preached after his death. We know this because the Apostles kept the Law and refused to mix with the Gentiles. See Acts 10:28, where Peter said it was unlawful for Jews to keep company with a Gentile, and in 21:17-26, the Apostles and thousands of believers were still keeping apart from the Gentiles and worshiping with the Jews. The passages such as Acts chapters 10 & 11 where the Apostles supposedly received the Holy Ghost and accepted the conversion of the Gentiles are Church fabrications. Because after the Apostles called Paul onto the carpet in Galatians 2 and Acts 15:1-21 they still recognized the believing Gentiles as only being under the Law of Noah, the divine Law considered to have been in operation prior to the Covenant of Moses (Acts 15:19-20), and inferred that they still needed to accept the Law of Moses (v. 21).

This also proves false the story in Luke 7:1-10 of the centurion's ill servant. Jesus would never have associated with a Gentile, especially a Roman soldier. To do so would have conflicted with his teachings. We have already mentioned the incident in which he referred to the gentile woman as a "dog." Association with Gentiles was a violation of the Jewish Law because the Gentiles touched and ate the unclean, and if a Jew touched a contaminated object, even unknowingly, he was unclean and had to make offerings and undergo a cleansing process. The Jews were fanatical about the subject, so much so rabbis have been known to sit around for days and weeks pondering such puzzles as to when an object becomes contaminated. For instance: If holy water is poured into an unclean cup when does it become unclean? Is it contaminated after all enters the cup, or does the contamination run up the stream and into the clean cup? This was one reason Jesus condemned the Pharisees and Sadducees so harshly. They were not only flaunting the Law, but were fraternizing with the enemy—the Romans. And Luke's explanation that the Jewish elders vouched for the centurion because he built a synagogue for them further contradicts the story. The elders were members of the council, Sadducees and Pharisee, the same people Jesus called "hypocrites" and "whited sepulchers," what influence would they have had with Jesus?

Matthew Chapters 5-7 & Luke 6:20-49

The beautiful and stirring Sermon on the Mount, attributed to Jesus, is absent from Mark, which of course, indicates another late addition. While Matthew's version covers three chapters, Luke's is short and condensed with subjects such as the discourse on the Law omitted. Since we know the writer of Luke had access to Matthew the question as to why it wasn't copied more accurately is raised. Also the fact that Luke had access to Matthew eliminates the possibility that he was working from memory or oral tradition. Could it be that additions and interpolations expanded the discourse in Matthew after Luke was written? There is one passage in this section that raises another question concerning the date of its origin. In Matthew 5:17-18 Jesus strongly endorses the Law and even condemns any who might break one commandment.

> Think not that I am come to destroy the Law, or the prophets: I am not come to destroy, but to fulfill. For very I say unto you, Till heaven and earth pass, one jot or one tittle shall in no wise pass from the Law, till all be fulfilled.

But which Law was Jesus referring to? There was no Christianity, no writings, or a New Testament. Obviously, Jesus was referring to the Law of Moses—the Torah—because he mentioned it in conjunction with the prophets, showing that he meant all the teachings of the Old Testament. Of the Jewish sects, it was the Essenes and Pharisees who counted the prophets as equal to the Law of Moses. In fact, the Tanakh, the Hebrew Bible, consisting of three parts—the Law (Torah), the Prophets, and the Writings—was the only Law recognized by Jesus and the Jews. Pauline Christianity teaches that the Law was abolished by the death of Christ and that the believer keeps, or fulfills, the Law spiritually. Paul declared a salvation achieved by believing in the death and resurrection of Jesus Christ apart from deeds. But Jesus taught just the opposite—that the Law would be in force until "heaven and earth" passed away. The last time I noticed, the earth was still spinning along.

Some might point to Luke 16:16:

> The Law and the prophets were until John: since that time the kingdom of God is preached, and every man presseth into it.

Does this not say the Law ended with John? No, it says the Law and prophets were taught, or preached, until John came preaching the kingdom of God. What was both John and Jesus' message? Repent, for the kingdom of God is at hand. Still in doubt? Look at verse 17:

> And it is easier for heaven and earth to pass, than one tittle of the Law to fail.

This is the same message as in Matthew. Notice that the second part of Jesus' statement in Matthew was a promise:

> Whosoever therefore shall break one of these least commandments, and shall teach men so, he shall be called

the least in the kingdom of heaven: but whosoever shall do and teach, the same shall be called great in the kingdom of heaven. (Matt. 5:19)

This is the same Law referred to in Deuteronomy 4:2:

You shall not add unto the word which I command you, neither shall ye diminish ought from it, that ye may keep the commandments of the Lord your God which I command you.

It is the same Law, of which Jesus was speaking. Given to the Jews, you say, and not meant for the Gentiles. Look at Micah 4:1&2:

But in the last days it shall come to pass, that the mountain of the house of the Lord shall be established in the top of the mountains, and it shall be exalted above the hills; and people shall flow unto it. And many nations shall come, and say, Come, and let us go up to the mountain of the Lord, and to the house of the God of Jacob; and he will teach us of his ways, and we will walk in his paths: for the Law shall go forth of Zion, and the word of the Lord from Jerusalem.

Of course Christianity teaches that Jesus did away with the literal observance of the Law and expanded upon it by requiring a spiritual observance as noted in the following verses of Matthew. No longer was murder limited to the taking of a life, violent anger might also condemn a man. Offerings alone would not be sufficient. Lust and adultery might be committed within the heart. An eye for an eye was to be replaced by submission. Love of one's enemies was commanded. This world was to be held in disdain while a desire for the coming kingdom was encouraged. Although Jesus seems to be instituting a new approach to observing the Law it conflicts with the Jewish teachings to which he strictly adhered, and raises some unanswered questions. First, of course, is that of his Apostles' doctrines. We must assume that they were present and heard Jesus' new instructions, and we should also assume that they were as intelligent as the average listener, therefore, capable of understanding these new teachings. Why then, were they continuing to observe the Law years later when they confronted Paul? The excuse that the new salvation was only revealed later by a risen Jesus won't stand if we accept this passage, because according to it, Jesus was already introducing new doctrines. Secondly, in Matthew 15:11, Jesus allegedly said:

Not that which goeth into the mouth defileth a man; but that which cometh out of the mouth, this defilith a man.

Jesus goes on to explain this statement, making sure his disciples understand, and yet years later, before Peter's visit to Cornelius, a Gentile, he needs a vision from God to clear his confused mind. If Jesus did speak the verse above, and thereby introduce a spiritual observance of the Law, then he failed to get that point across to his disciples, and all the time and effort he spent in choosing and training them was wasted because they never ceased to keep the letter of the Law. In fact, they contented with Paul throughout his entire ministry on such issues as circumcision and cleanliness. It was Paul who introduced the idea of a spiritual kingdom and salvation through a risen Jesus Christ. He said he learned nothing from men, and received his enlightenment from Jesus Christ, the Son of God (Galatians 1:11&12). Read Paul's writings. His are the only works we can date with any degree of accuracy (during the 50s CE) and at that time he was preaching the changes and claiming them as his own. If they had been given by Jesus earlier why weren't the Apostles teaching them?

The Sermon on the Mount is a beautiful discourse, powerful, direct, and concise, one that any theologian would be proud to have authored. The instructions in righteousness, piety, tolerance, self-sacrifice, trust, and meekness are admirable, but stressed to the point of foolishness. They are fine moral values when used with common sense and moderation, but as instructed here they become a steel rod for a controlling and dictating Church: a Church that demanded utter control and booked no dissensions, a Church that brainwashed and enslaved its members, and, in later years, tortured or slaughtered those it labeled heretics.

These instructions deny a man his dignity, pride, and initiative while stripping him of his ability to reason. In short, he is reduced to a zombie-like being that is to accept and obey what he is told. Church history reveals that the common man was deprived education and kept in the darkness of ignorance. Let's dissect some of these directives:

And whosoever shall compel thee to go a mile, go with him twain. Give to him that askth thee, and from him that would borrow of thee turn not thou away. (Matt. 5:41&42)

Where is the logic of this statement? Are we to teach our children to go willingly with anyone who approaches them in the mall and takes their hand? If I loan my neighbor my lawn mower and he never returns it, wouldn't I be a fool to lend him my weed-eater? What the Church wanted at that time was a large number of fools who would obey blindly and pay their tithes. For proof:

> Therefore I say unto you. Take no thought for your life, what ye shall eat, or what ye shall drink; nor yet for your body, what ye shall put on. Is not life more than meat, and the body than raiment: Behold the fowls of the air; for they sow not, neither do they reap, nor gather into barns; yet your heavenly Father feedeth them. Are ye not much better than they? (Matt. 6:25&26)

> Therefore take no thought, saying, "What shall we eat?" or, "What shall we drink?" or "Wherewithal shall we be clothed?" (Matt. 6:31)

> Take therefore no thought for the morrow: for the morrow shall take thought for the things of itself. Sufficient unto the day is the evil thereof. (Matt. 6:34)

I'm aware that the Church today doesn't interpret these passages literally—that the intent is to contrast the things of this world to the kingdom to come. But that wasn't the original purpose of these teachings. These ideas most assuredly originated through oral tradition when the early believers were expecting the immediate coming kingdom on earth (See Acts 5 where Peter pronounced a curse of death on Ananias and Sapphira). Later, when the kingdom tarried and the Church became more powerful they were used as a rod to control the masses. Don't worry. Don't ask questions. Just do as you're told, pay your tithes and we'll pray God's blessing upon you. A message of dependency that sounded good in a theocratic society expecting the end of the age, but a recipe for financial disaster and enslavement in the real world.

Matthew 12:14&24, Mark 3:6-22 & Luke 11:14

Of the Synoptic Gospels, Matthew is the most Jewish in that the writer keeps trying to depict Jesus as the fulfillment of Hebraic

Scripture and makes references to Jewish Law and customs. In this passage we have another futile attempt to find a reference to Jesus in the book of Isaiah. Jesus had just perceived that the Pharisees were plotting to destroy him and a great multitude followed as he was leaving. He healed them all and charges them not to make him known.

> That it might be fulfilled which was spoken by Esaias the prophet, saying, "Behold my servant, whom I have chosen; my beloved, in whom my soul is well pleased: I will put my spirit upon him, and he shall shew judgment to the Gentiles. He shall not strive, nor cry; neither shall any man hear his voice in the streets. A bruised reed shall he not break, and smoking flax shall he not quench, till he send forth judgment unto victory. And in his name shall the Gentiles trust."

Matthew 12:14-21 is supposed to be a fulfillment of this prophecy. This certainly appears to fore tell the introduction and worldwide appeal of Christianity. However, we must not forget that the Gospels postdated the events, so this would not be a prediction, but an equivocation. In addition, when studying the Gospels, never forget they were written or translated by Gentiles—most likely Hellenistic Jews—who had no compulsions about taking liberties in doing so. One should also remember that Jesus had nothing to do with the Gentiles; it was Paul who carried the *gospel* to them.

Whatever the reason, it makes little difference because Isaiah wasn't referring to Jesus, or even a Jewish messiah. There are four passages in Isaiah chapters 42-53 commonly referred to as *servant songs*. Today, many Christian writers admit that the servant in this passage refers to Cyrus the Persian who overthrew the Babylonians and freed the Israelites.

Isaiah 42:2 says "he shall not cry, nor cause his voice to be heard in the streets." This appears to mean the servant would be a man of actions instead of words. This doesn't apply to Jesus because he was certainly making his voice heard, to such an extent the Pharisees were seeking means to destroy him.

What follows is a confusion of tales and parables. After Jesus is accused of casting out devils by Beelzebub he delivers his kingdom divided sermon then everything becomes pandemonium. Again, Mark is simple and straightforward, the statement is short. It points out that a house, kingdom, or even Satan cannot stand if divided. It states that blasphemies will be forgiven except those against the Holy Ghost. Then Jesus' brothers and mother come calling for him, and he identifies those who follow him as his mother and brothers. Chapter three ends and chapter four opens with a scene change to the seaside.

Apparently the writer of Matthew was the forerunner of some of the ministers I've heard in my time who could read one verse and build it up into a novel. He tosses in a metaphor of a corrupt tree bearing corrupt fruit, then launches into a diatribe about a generation of vipers speaking evil, and warns that they will be judged by every word spoken. The scribes and Pharisees sought a sign, which gave the writer a chance to slip in a post-dated prophecy that referred to Jonah's three days in the fish's belly and was suppose to be symbolic of Jesus spending three days and nights in the grave. Next the writer throws in an end time prophecy about a queen of the south and an unclean spirit searching for roommates. Then he comes back to the thread of events described by Mark.

In Luke it's hard to follow the events. Apparently the writer wanted to insert a tale he'd heard, or invented, of a female listener blessing Jesus' mother, so he slipped the Pharisee's request for a sign in prior to the discourse. Afterward he followed Matthew's outline until he came to the reference to Jonah. Here the writer doesn't mention the three days and nights, he merrily compares Jesus' preaching to that of Jonah. He also omits the queen of the south and the wicked spirits. Instead, he introduces the metaphors of the candle under a bushel and the light of the eye.

It has been determined that the Gospels are simply collections of orally repeated stories and parables that the writers tried to arrange in a coherent and logical series of events. Their efforts were in vain. Originally, the events were told or recorded as separate stories before being collected and grouped in book form. The events described are bridged by contrived comments or leading questions such as those of the Pharisees and the woman just mentioned. The result is a series of disjointed tales, with little continuity, that are impossible to follow. And where one gospel writer records the events in one manner, another places them in another order. Also, as can be seen, one writer would discount certain statements while adding others he considered more favorable or pertinent. For example: in Matthew and Mark the series of events following these passages in question, track a similar outline, but Luke seems to have little regard for continuity. There, the same events revert back to chapter eight where they occur before the events just described.

Matthew 16:13-19, Mark 8:27-29 & Luke 9:18-21

Looking at these passages, I would like to remind you that the word *Christ* is the Greek translation of the Hebrew word, *Messiah*. Paul is the first writer to teach the doctrine of a risen Christ as opposed to a messiah, about two to three years after Jesus' ministry, and he claimed it originated with him (Galatians 1:11&12). So, if Peter recognized Jesus as the *Christ* prior to Paul's *revelation* of him (Matthew 16:16), he was, in actuality, saying Jesus was the *Messiah*. We have also shown that the doctrine of a personal savior would have been in direct opposition to Jesus' explicit teaching on the Law and salvation. Jesus did perceive himself as the Messiah, but in actuality he would not have taught that he was the Son of God in a divine sense.

If we compare Jesus' teachings with those of the Essenes it becomes obvious that they are very similar. The Essenes waited expectantly for the kingdom of God. When the signs were right, they were to send forth prophets to warn the people of Israel, calling them to repentance. That this point was reached is made evident by the message of the Kingdom, preached by John the Baptist and Jesus. What they taught along with that message had been lost or distorted until the revelation of the Dead Sea scrolls. Those scrolls give us a great understanding of their doctrines and expectations.

Though the Essenes sought perfection, they did not believe it could be obtained on earth in their mortal forms. Their philosophy was that if it was of this world, it was subject to error. That included their predictions. They could discern the times and signs, but there was no guarantee their predictions would be right. Therefore, when the diviners of the signs considered the end time was near, a nasi, a leader or ruler, was to be sent out into the community to test the attitude of the people. He would tell them of the coming kingdom and call them to repentance. This safeguarded the Essenes as a whole while allowing God to show whether the signs were correct or not.

Most likely, John the Baptist was one such leader, Jesus was his heir—the *nasi*, the prince, the leader of a vanguard whose duty was to mobilize the rank and file. Accordingly, his converts were called Nazarenes—followers of the nasi. This explains why the followers of John the Baptist were also called Nazarenes. The nasi might or might not be the messiah, that depended upon God. He was simply the leader of the congregation of Israel in the last days, but the Semitic root nsr, meaning protector or savior, suggests that by God's will he would become the messiah.

In the Essenes' *Commentary on Nahum* it explains that the ranks of the believers would be expanded, prior to the battle with the sons of darkness, by the conversion of the wayward Jews. As the kingdom drew nigh the number of such converts were expected to mushroom as the new covenant attracted the lost sheep of the house of Israel back to the fold. The phrase, all the congregation of Israel, implies that many Jews were expected to return to the fold by the end time. So, when Jesus asked his disciples, "Whom do men say that I am?" he was most likely trying to ascertain if God had chosen him as the Messiah. The people only viewed him as a prophet, but it was Peter who spoke the words he obviously longed to hear. "Thou art the Messiah."

This also explains why Jesus instructed them to "... tell no man of him." If the people were to recognize Jesus as the Messiah it was to be a revelation of God—not one instilled by his followers. This is substantiated by the remark he made to Peter. "Blessed art thou, Simon Barjona: for flesh and blood hath not revealed it unto thee, but my Father which is in heaven." The same revelation had to be made to all who would believe. It had to come from God, not man. And what of the play upon *Peter*, the rock, the foundation of the church, meaning the congregation? Peter was obviously the first one to speak the words Jesus waited to hear. The foundation of Jesus' ministry would have been his acceptance as the Messiah—not Peter's perception.

It was probably then, that Jesus first believed he was the Messiah, for from that time he began to promote himself as that *savior* with remarks such as:

> For whosoever will save his life shall lose it: and whosoever will lose his life for my sake shall find it. (Mk. 8:35)

Then he speaks of the Son of man's return in glory and promises the kingdom within the lifetime of some of those present. The Essenes believed that when the times were right God would change the nasi into the messiah, and when the kingdom appeared men would be transformed into angels. The first would be the nasi who would become the archangel Michael. This would explain the Nazarenes' expectation of Jesus' return—he was the first transformed. Or as Paul later phrased it, "But now is Christ risen from the dead and become the first-fruits of them that slept" (I Corinthians 15:20).

Matthew 17:1-23, Mark 9:2-10, 31-32 & Luke 9:28-36, 44-45

Here we have three accounts of the transfiguration and Jesus' prediction of his death and resurrection. What are we to make of this … what … hallucination? Is this the point at which Jesus became the Son of God—the Christ—who would draw the Gentiles to himself? Or was it symbolic of what was to occur at his resurrection? No matter, it has to be an interpolation because if the Apostles had experienced such a marvelous teaching aid they would have been preaching to the Gentiles before Paul ever came on the scene. Come on! You don't hear the voice of God and not get the message. At least, I don't suppose I would.

The Gospels repeatedly depict Jesus as teaching of his death, yet the disciples were ignorant of any such event (John 20:9). And, the entire story is simply ridiculous. However, we do find one small grain of truth where Jesus refers to his resurrection on the third day. According to Essene belief the righteous would be raised up (with incorruptible bodies) in the kingdom of God on the third day of the kingdom in accordance with Hosea 6:2. Here can be seen the root of the Christian belief of Jesus' resurrection on the third day, and the spiritual resurrection of the soul in heaven. More than likely this was what Jesus was teaching before it was Christianized.

Matt. 19:16-24, Mk. 10:17-25 & Lu. 18:18-25

For years I used these Scriptures to prove that Jesus taught obedience to the Law when the opposite is true. A young man, or a lawyer—which is hard to discern—presumably a Jew, came to Jesus asking what he must do to obtain eternal life. Jesus' told him to keep the Commandments, and quoted some of those Commandments. My understanding was that he gave the quotes to further identify the Law. What I failed to see was that Jesus was not identifying the Ten Commandments, but listing only the ones that mattered to the Gentiles. Notice that the five missing commandments are lumped under one—a new commandment: *Thou shalt love thy neighbor as thyself.* Even more interesting is the five that are missing: *You shall have no other gods before me. You shall not make for yourself a carved image. You shall not take the name of the Lord your God in vain. Remember the Sabbath day, to keep it holy. Honor your father and your mother.* Notice the one thing these omitted commandments have in common—they are all germane to Jewish observance of the Law, but impossible for Paul's gentile converts to keep without converting to Judaism.

In these passages, we find Jesus teaching this amazing new doctrine, even before his resurrection, but was this the first time this concept was recorded? No. Remember, in an earlier article we saw that Paul's works, written about 50-60 CE, were the earliest New Testament writings and that the Gospels were written from 60 to 110 CE. That means all the Gospels were written after the fact—therefore, they could be and were written or altered to enforce Christian beliefs. Here is a perfect example. Let's see just were this alteration of the Ten Commandments originated.

> For this, Thou shalt not commit adultery, Thou shalt not kill, Thou shalt not steal, Thou shalt not bear false witness, Thou shalt not covet; and if there be any other commandment, it is briefly comprehended in this saying, namely, Thou shalt love thy neighbour as thyself. (Rom. 13:9)

Here is the first recorded use of this teaching—by Paul, not Jesus—written perhaps forty years before the Gospels, yet after Jesus' death. But wait, couldn't Jesus have actually spoken these words? No, because they contradict the Law and other teachings of Jesus. When Moses delivered the Ten Commandments to the Israelites God commanded:

> And now, Israel, what doth the LORD thy God require of thee, but to fear the LORD thy God, to walk in all his ways, and to love

him, and to serve the LORD thy God with all thy heart and with all thy soul,

To keep the commandments of the LORD, and his statutes, which I command thee this day for thy good? (Deu. 10:12-13)

Therefore thou shalt love the LORD thy God, and keep his charge, and his statutes, and his judgments, and his commandments, *alway [Emphasis added]*. (Deu. 11:1)

And let's not forget that passage in Matthew 5 that assures the eternity of the Law:

Think not that I am come to destroy the law, or the prophets: I am not come to destroy, but to fulfil. For verily I say unto you, Till heaven and earth pass, one jot or one tittle shall in no wise pass from the law, till all be fulfilled. Whosoever therefore shall break one of these least commandments, and shall teach men so, he shall be called the least in the kingdom of heaven: but whosoever shall do and teach [them], the same shall be called great in the kingdom of heaven (Matthew 5:17-19).

These were words spoken by Jesus, a direct contradiction to Paul's gospel. I've no idea how they survived the censoring quills, but it leaves no doubt God never sanctioned Paul's new plan of salvation.

We also have two points in these passages that enforce the idea that Jesus was connected with the Essenes. One is Jesus' disdain for riches. When Jesus told the rich, young man he must give away all his wealth the young man was unable to part with it. The Essene believers equated wealth with sin, and hated the rich. Wealth was one of the three major sins of Belial. It was the rich who deceived the people and led them from the precepts of God. In contrast, they called themselves the Poor. In their *War Scroll*, following a prophecy of the kingdom, is written:

... by the hand of the Poor whom you have redeemed by Your Power and the peace of Your Mighty Wonders... by the hand of the Poor and those bent in the dust, You will deliver the enemies of all the lands and humble the mighty of the peoples to bring upon their heads the reward of the Wicked and justify the Judgment of Your Truth on all the sons of men.

In James 2:3 the author fired off an angry salvo against the rich, condemning them forthright without regard to personal merit. Why? Remember the deaths of Ananias and Sapphira in Acts 5 when the *Christians* were awaiting the return of Jesus? Those believers were, in actuality, the Nazarenes (Jewish followers of Jesus) awaiting the return of their Messiah. God had chosen the poor and promised the kingdom to them. The rich oppressed the poor and brought them before the judgment seat. This is a teaching that Christians today want to deny. In the passage above, we have the story of a rich young man who wanted eternal life. Jesus told him he must keep the commandments, the Law of Moses, to which the young man affirmed that he had. For the orthodox Jew, this would have been sufficient, but Jesus required more. According to Essene belief eternal life was gained upon entry into the soon coming kingdom of God. To enter it the young man had to denounce the rich and give his wealth to the poor—the Essenes. Matthew 18:21 makes it even more explicit, "If thou wouldst be perfect, go, sell that thou hast." We see this in practice by Jesus' followers in Acts 4:32-5:11. The Essenes also called themselves The Perfect.

And the second point: of the four prevalent religious philosophies identified by Josephus, the Sadducees, Pharisees, Essenes, and Zealots, the Gospels make it doubtful that Jesus could have been of the first two persuasions. When Mark writes in 1:22 that Jesus was teaching not as the scribes, he is virtually admitting that he was an Essene or a Zealot. The scribes were mainly Pharisees. Most of the priests were Sadducees, who had little philosophy other than the atoning sacrifices of temple worship, and they would never have spoken against the status quo with which they were entirely satisfied. Of Josephus's four philosophies, only the Essenes and the Zealots are left. From the Qumran literature, it is evident that the Essenes were fanatics for the establishment of the kingdom of God on earth. From Josephus we find that the Zealots also were fanatics for the kingdom of God on earth, and actually fought for it. The Gospels tell us that Jesus opposed scribes, Pharisees, priests and Sadducees, but taught of the imminence of God's kingdom. In all likelihood Jesus was an Essene, if not, he was well acquainted with, and taught, their doctrines.

Matthew 22:1-46, Mark 11:1-12:12, Luke 19:1-48

All three Synoptic Gospels convey the story of Jesus' triumphant entry into Jerusalem, and all three agree emphatically that Jesus was viewed as the Messiah, not a spiritual, personal redeemer. That Jesus considered himself the Messiah is evident by the fact he endeavored to fulfill the prophecy in Zechariah 9:9, which states explicitly that the king would ride into Jerusalem on a foal. By doing so, Jesus was stating—*I am the king!* In Luke 19:10 Jesus says, "… the Son of man is come to seek and save that which was lost." When the people heard this, and because Jesus was near Jerusalem, they thought the Kingdom of God was imminent. And they welcomed him as the King (Luke 19:38). What occurred should be obvious. When Jesus rode into Jerusalem on Palm Sunday he was viewed as the Messiah. And it doesn't matter whether he was at the head of an army or not, the people rose up and by sheer numbers took the temple.

At the head of that army of citizens Jesus stormed into the temple and turned over the tables of the money changers, ran the buyers and sellers out, and controlled passage through. It's impossible to determine if he expected the holy army of God to descend at that time or not, but that action sealed his fate. Jesus obviously had control because the High Priests normally had absolute power over the temple, and there were guards who would have thrown Jesus out or arrested him under normal conditions. Instead the priests simply asked him by whose authority he acted—to eliminate the possibility that he was acting under Roman authority. If we assume they were only allowing him to incriminate himself, they would still have arrested him at some point. Instead, he occupied the temple and taught daily, which implies he had control for a number of days. Mark 11:17-18 and Matthew 26:3-5 state that the scribes and priests desired to kill him but feared the people.

Matthew 24- 26:1-5, Mark 13-14:1-2, Luke 21-22:1-2

We might assume that as the days passed, Jesus taught and debated within the temple while he awaited the army of God.

But crowds are ruled by emotions, not reason, and as the days passed and the kingdom tarried it appears the people drifted away to attend the business of daily life. Eventually, Jesus left the temple and the priests were waiting.

As Jesus and his disciples left the temple, they were admiring the structure. It was then that Jesus revealed he still believed in the coming kingdom, "… the days will come in the which there shall not be left one stone upon another, that shall not be thrown down." This was one of the Essenes central beliefs, that the temple was defiled and must be destroyed. But later writers have inserted an end time revelation depicting the destruction of Jerusalem in 70 CE by the Romans. Or, as some end time evangelical sects preach, an end of the world scenario. The fact that none of the Gospels were written until after Jerusalem fell made it easy to post-date history.

The chief priest and scribes still saw Jesus as a threat and sought to destroy him, but they had to do it in a manner that would not discredit them in the eyes of the people. The story of Judas' betrayal is suspect. Why his aid would be necessary is unclear. Since Jesus taught openly in the temple his identity should not have been in question. Luke 22:6 says they sought an opportunity when the multitude was absent. However, if such was the case, why would they put him on trial and make a huge public spectacle of the situation? Because he had to be discredited openly and publicly.

Matthew 26:47-27:61, Mark 14:43-15:41, Luke 22:47-23:56

Little, if any, of the tales surrounding Jesus' trial and crucifixion can be accounted creditable because they contradict the Judaic Law and teachings that Jesus advocated so strongly. For instance, in Matthew 26:31-32 & Mark 14:27-28, Jesus predicts his death and resurrection, and tells the disciples he will meet them in Galilee. Yet in the resurrection events the disciples couldn't believe such a tale even after the women reminded them. And the tales of the high priests pleading with Pilate to kill Jesus, and Pilate's reluctance, doesn't conform to reality. In one instance, the Romans crucified about two thousand dissidents following a rebellion, why would one loony, self-proclaimed messiah merit Pilate's attention?

Josephus made references to a number of not so well-known people of his era, including Jewish false messiahs and cult leaders. One was Theudas, who recruited some thousands of followers and brought them to the banks of the Jordan in the belief the river would open to facilitate their triumphal march on Jerusalem. Another was the Egyptian, mentioned in Acts 21:38, who led a body of partisans as far as the Mount of Olives, convinced the walls of Jerusalem would fall down. Yet, Josephus had very little to say regarding Jesus. In fact, the secular world, including Rome, seems to have scarcely heard of him other than through the highly lauded tales produced by Christianity. Surely, if all the excitement surrounding Jesus' trial, crucifixion, the resurrection of a God, the dead rising and walking about town, and the founding of a new religion had occurred wouldn't it have had a prominent place in Josephus' writings? This indicates that Jesus' ministry, apprehension, and crucifixion were either a short-lived nuisance to Roman authority, has been the subject of a massive cover-up, or never occurred.

That there were animosity and dissension by the Sadducees toward Jesus is evident in the fact that Jesus was brought to trial before the High Priest. (Mark has him on trial before the Sanhedrin, but even many Christian commentators think that story is fictional.) Obviously he did something, but what? The Sadducees were irate because he took control of the temple and disrupted traffic, but was that a criminal offense that befitted death? Yes, but by Roman law! According to it, by assuming the power of civic authorities and controlling passage through the temple he had committed the crime of *Laesae Majestatis*. Of this he was definitely guilty because he overthrew the tables and refused to allow anyone to carry anything through.

But was Jesus guilty? Was he an insurrectionist? In Matthew 10:34 Jesus told his followers that he had not come to send peace on the earth, but a sword. Plainly meaning the coming struggle to route the Romans and usher in the kingdom of God. In Luke he said he would cast fire on the earth and the kingdom had to be entered violently. In Luke 22:36 he urges his followers to buy swords, on credit if possible or, if necessary, by selling their clothes. Luke tries to make it appear that Jesus wanted the weapons to deliberately break the Law to fulfill prophecy (Isaiah 53:12) but since he'd already broken the Law such reasoning is senseless.

In Luke 13:1-5 some come to Jesus telling him of Pilate (meaning his soldiers) mingling the blood of Galileans with their sacrifice, which might refer to a Sabbath attack by the Romans, against rebels within the temple. Jesus answered by mentioning eighteen upon whom the tower of Siloam fell. He then used both cases to urge repentance less his listeners perish likewise. Why? How would repentance preserve them from the Romans—unless that repentance was, like the Essenes' teachings, a commitment to arms?

The strongest evidence that Jesus was an insurrectionist is the fact that he was crucified as one, and the proof of that fact is recorded in the Gospels. Herman Samuel Reimarus, a Hamburg language professor writing two hundred years ago pointed out there was one Jesus, a freedom fighter leading a revolution against the Romans. He listed gospel evidence as this:

- He gathered large crowds which the authorities considered potentially subversive.
- He was described as a Galilaean, like Judas the Galilaean, a rebel.
- The nickname of many of his followers sounded more like men of violence than men of peace. (That is: Petra, meaning Rocky, the tempestuous brothers and the Sons of Thunder.)
- He deliberately depicted himself as a king as he entered Jerusalem and his supporters greeted him as such openly.
- He had committed the crime in Roman Law of Laesae Majestatis by assuming the power of civic authorities to deny passage through the temple.
- An insurrection had occurred in which men had died and Jesus' supporters had been armed and resisted arrest with violence, cutting off a man's ear.
- When Jesus was charged as a rival to Caesar's rule in Judea, claiming to be the king of the Jews, he chose not to deny it unequivocally at his trial.
- Jesus was Barabbas, the nasi, one of the holy ones of God but a failed rebel.

Reimarus' reference to Jesus being Barabbas comes from the Aramaic meaning of Barabbas, which is Son of my Father. Jesus always called God, my father, using the Aramaic term Abba. Therefore Jesus' title, Son of God, could be interpreted Barabbas. According to

Origin, an early Church writer, some old manuscripts of Matthew reveal the full name of the criminal as Jesus Barabbas.

I believe we've revealed more than sufficient evidence to ascertain that Jesus was a leader in a rebellion to drive the Romans from his country. I know that the idea of Jesus with a sword in his hand is abhorrent to Christians today. But it shouldn't be. Why is it so hard to envision Jesus fighting the Gentiles to preserve Judaism and the Law of God when the Christian Church exterminated millions of *heretics* in his name to preserve the power of their dogma? In the Catholic Encyclopedia they cite Jesus, Paul and the Apostles as authority for their atrocities. And there can be no mistaking their intent.

> The apostles acted upon their Master's directions. All the weight of their own Divine faith and mission is brought to bear upon innovators. "If any one," says St. Paul, "preach to you a gospel, besides that you have received, let him be anathema" (Galatians 1:9). To St. John the heretic is a seducer, an antichrist, a man who dissolves Christ (1 John 4:3; 2 John 7); "receive him not into the house nor say to him, God speed you" (II John, 10). St. Peter, true to his office and to his impetuous nature, assails them as with a two-edged sword: " ... lying teachers who shall bring in sects of perdition, and deny the Lord who bought them: bringing upon themselves swift destruction. ... These are fountains without water, and clouds tossed with whirlwinds, to whom the mist of darkness is reserved" (2 Peter 2:1, 17). St. Jude speaks in a similar strain throughout his whole epistle. St. Paul admonishes the disturbers of the unity of faith at Corinth that "the weapons of our warfare .... are mighty to God unto the pulling down of fortifications, destroying counsels, and every height that exalteth itself against the knowledge of God ... and having in readiness to revenge all disobedience" (2 Corinthians 10:4, 5, 6). https://www.ecatholic2000.com/cathopedia/vol7/volseven300.shtml

Christianity teaches that Christ died for all mankind. No one is forced to serve God; man is a free agent. However, in the past, if you chose not to believe the Church, you were a heretic, an antichrist, and were to be exterminated. It was a case of bow the knee or offer the neck. But the poor wretch shouldn't be concerned; either way, God loved him. Though the Church spoke of love and forgiveness, their affections were the same as those of the Old Testament God. They were reserved only for those who submitted to their God. The

Church even claimed a divine blessing from God to stamp out all opposition. It was a matter of natural survival!

> The first Law of life, be it the life of plant or animal, of man or of a society of men, is self-preservation... The integrity of the rule of faith is more essential to the cohesion of a religious society than the strict practice of its moral precepts. For faith supplies the means of mending moral delinquencies as one of its ordinary functions, whereas the loss of faith, cutting at the root of spiritual life, is usually fatal to the soul... The jealousy with which the Church guards and defends her deposit of faith is therefore identical with the instinctive duty of self-preservation and the desire to live...In the Catholic Church this natural Law has received the **sanction of Divine promulgation**, as appears from the teaching of Christ and the apostles quoted above... (New Advent Catholic Encyclopedia - https://www.ecatholic2000. com/cathopedia/vol7/volseven300.shtml **(Emphasis added)**.

Considering the blood-lust and hatred of the early Christians toward heretics, and their zeal in stamping out any conflicting doctrines, why should it be so hard to believe that Jesus was a religious freedom fighter? But whether such is so or not, Jesus was certainly guilty under the civil law of Rome. How the crucifixion was carried out is of little importance. So many tales have been spun about the event that there's no way the truth could ever be revealed. It is enough to know that Pilate found him guilty of insurrection and passed the only sentence possible under the conditions. It is almost a certainty he was crucified. What happened to his body afterwards is impossible to ascertain.

But if his crime was only against the Romans, why was he brought to trial before the Jewish court? First we have to understand the social situation. Jesus and the excited masses controlled the temple. Outside the city, the Romans were probably readying a force to assault the temple and capture him. Of course the Sadducees, who operated the temple and were collaborating with the Romans, wanted him out. The Pharisees were more concerned with the welfare of the populace. But whatever their motives and political leanings, all the Jewish leaders knew how the Romans would react. On previous occasions they had put down rebellions by slaughtering thousands of Jewish citizens. With this in mind, let's look at a comment made by the high priest, Caiaphas, in John 18:14.

"Now Caiaphas was he, which gave counsel to the Jews, that it was expedient that one man should die for the people."

This explains a great deal. The Jewish leaders, either through disbelief in Jesus as the Messiah or common sense, realized God's army of holy angels was not going to appear. So, to avert a massacre of the people they believed it best to surrender Jesus. This also provides an answer to why they were so anxious to find fault with him. They were afraid to pass sentence upon an innocent man because the people were still agitated. And for the same reason they were reluctant to turn him over to the Romans. They needed to find him guilty of breaking the Jewish Law. It would also explain why we find Jesus' disciples worshiping with the Jews years later. They held no malice toward the Jews because they had acted to save lives.

Matthew 27:62-28:20, Mark 16, Luke 24:1-53

Any sensible man should judge resurrection stories as ludicrous based simply on their subject, but in Christian circles such will not suffice. Therefore, we must look at the evidence or, in this case, lack of evidence. To do so we must turn to the differing resurrection stories. As mentioned previously, Mark's final chapter concerning the resurrection was a late addition not found in the earliest manuscripts and should be labeled false. Another indication that chapter sixteen is at least out of sequence is the second mention of the two Mary's after just referring to them at the end of chapter fifteen (Note: the original texts were not divided into chapters.). Other inconsistencies and contradictions identify the tales as nothing more than fables. In Mark the stone is already rolled away and a man in white garment is awaiting the women when they arrive at the sepulcher. In Matthew there are two women, an earthquake and an angel to roll back the stone. In Luke there is a group of women and two men in white with a reminder that Jesus had already told them of his crucifixion and resurrection. An obvious Church addition, since we've already learned the Apostles knew nothing about it.

Again, we see the growth and exaggeration from earlier to later Gospels. Mark records only a man in the empty tomb. The resurrection tale is added later. In Matthew there is an earthquake and the man has become an angel. To prove the body wasn't simply stolen, guards are set and a cover-up is hatched. And to sanction the ministry to the Gentiles both Mark and Matthew have a resurrected Jesus sending the disciples to all the world. The incident in Mark is in the falsified last chapter, which attests to its credibility. In Mark and Matthew the women are instructed to tell the disciples to go to Galilee where they will see Jesus, yet before they can even pass the word, Jesus is already making appearances. From there through the Gospel of John the stories of Christ appearances pop-up like UFO sightings. And with almost every occurrence, Jesus institutes or endorses a controversial, gentile, Christian teaching. The impression one gets is that Jesus died a Jew and was resurrected a Gentile preaching newly discovered Christian doctrines. The obvious conclusion is that these passages were inserted years later to give credence to contested Church doctrines.

There is another set of puzzling incidents concerning the resurrection. In Mk. 14:28, Jesus says he'll appear to them in Galilee. This is repeated by the angel in Matt. 28:7, yet he first appeared to Mary near the sepulcher, then near Emmanus, a small village about seven miles from Jerusalem. And finally, he appeared to the disciples in Jerusalem—if you follow Luke or John—but Matthew puts the meeting in Galilee.

Many see a man—even those closest to Jesus—but don't recognize him. This includes the two at Emmanus who, incidentally, knew him as "Jesus of Nazareth, which was a prophet mighty in deed and word before God and all the people," not the son of God. Notice how he conveniently began teaching things that were omitted or overlooked during his earthly ministry—like a ministry to the Gentiles.

And referring to the disciples on the sea of Tiberias (John 21:1); notice how the beloved disciple seemingly cast a hypnotic trance over the others. They were fishing and a man hailed them from the shore: Have you caught anything? Then he told them to cast their net on the right side. When they did so it was full to bursting. Immediately "the disciple whom Jesus loved" said unto Peter, "It is the Lord." The suggestion was so powerful that later, as they were eating, none of the other disciples dared ask the man his name because they knew it was the Lord. Obviously, the man didn't look like Jesus or the question of his identity would have never arisen. It was only the huge haul of fish and the suggestion of John, the beloved disciple, which planted the idea of the stranger being Jesus.

While it's only logical that there be confusion about the stories, caused by the time lag between the occurrences and the recording of the events, it should be inconceivable that they were not altered by the Church during the subsequent years when no means were ignored if they served the Church's purpose. Though the New Testament is the basis for Catholic doctrines and the Christian beliefs of today, the true teachings of the Old Testament are still nestled in the under tones. One such example is evident in the remark made by the two at Emmanus. To them, Jesus was a mighty prophet, the messiah—not the Son of God.

All these convenient tidbits of truth are at variance with other scripture. As already pointed out, Peter certainly knew nothing about going to all nations. When the Apostles questioned Paul's ministry to the Gentiles, they obviously had no intentions of accepting his converts under the Law as long as they remained outside Judaism. In Acts 1:6 the Apostles ask the risen Jesus, "Lord, wilt thou at this time restore again the kingdom to Israel?" When that line was penned the mind-set was still that of a literal kingdom of God. In Acts 15:16 James, quoting from Amos 9:11, makes their position clear. The Davidic tabernacle would soon be rebuilt, and then all men would seek the Lord. Notice verses 19&20, the Gentiles were still not accepted under the Mosaic Law.

The only logical explanation for the missing body is that it was stolen from the tomb, but by whom? The man, or men, in white give us the strongest clue. The followers of John the Baptist and the Nazarenes, wore white and the Qumran Nasrani (Nazarenes) were called the people in white. Even modern Christianity pictures Jesus as dressed in white. Doesn't it stand to reason that the Essenes removed the body of one of their own for an honorable and proper burial? One even waited to inform Jesus' followers as to the actions taken with his body. Perhaps the confused message about him going before them to Galilee was simply directions to his final resting place.

The Essenes and the followers of Jesus believed the righteous would be raised from the dead on God's day of vengeance. When rumors of the empty tomb began circulating they came to the conclusion that Jesus had been resurrected as the first fruits of righteousness (See Revelation 1:5 and I Corinthians 15:20). Both Scriptures show that his followers thought the general resurrection had begun. More than likely, some thought they had seen Jesus.

Conclusion

I know if you are a true blue, dyed-in-the-wool, believing Christian, with unlimited faith, you are capable of tearing the arguments presented here to shreds; I could when I was a believing Christian. The pivotal point is faith. The Bible has a lot to say about faith. Or, perhaps I should say the New Testament has a lot to say about faith, it's only mentioned twice in the Old Testament. The word faithful is used repeatedly in the Old Testament in the sense of a duty, a faithful God, person, servant, witness, or messenger, all based on deeds or works whereby one might judge or be judged. For instance, a faithful servant would be one who served his master well, a faithful person speaks truthfully, and a faithful god keeps his word.

However, in the New Testament the Christian's concept of faith is denoted by an unsubstantiated belief. One is first asked to believe the person who introduces the Word—the messenger. Then they are asked to believe the message—the Bible (or for the most part, the New Testament). Next, they are asked to believe the storytellers, recorders, scribes, and compilers of that Bible. Lastly, they must believe that an unknowable, supernatural deity who cannot be evaluated, has miraculously preserved the integrity of his message. Only when we evaluate the enormity of this task can we perceive the priceless value of faith. To begin, let's consider the messenger, a parent, friend, minister or perhaps a stranger. Can we judge his integrity? Perhaps, if so, then the question of faith switches to the message. Where did the messenger get it? From a book or perhaps someone told him. Has he ascertained its truthfulness? Did he check its validity? No, if it could be rationally evaluated, there would be no need for faith. Obviously, he only believed the one who told him. And what was he told? That the book was written by holy men of old moved by the Holy Spirit. Did he prove that statement? No, but it's in the Bible, therefore it is true. But how can we be sure errors in selecting or copying haven't been made? Because the Holy Mother Church compiled the writings and the Church is infallible in such matters. But what of God, how can we know he is real? Because he said it and God cannot lie. Really, how do we know that? Because the Bible says God cannot lie.

In the end, the believer hasn't really been asked to believe the Bible, that there is a supreme deity, or in the death and resurrection of Jesus Christ. What the believer is asked to believe is the words of man. All these suppositions, and thousands of equally preposterous teachings, originated or passed through the hands of some unknown narrator or writer. While there is evidence that a man named Jesus may have existed, there is no proof to substantiate those ludicrous teachings. The only way to form a clear picture of the puzzle is to fill in the holes with generous amounts of faith.

AUTHENTICITY OF II PETER

Here is a story that strips the veneer from the New Testament book used to prove the validity of Christianity.

When the question of the Bible's authenticity arises, Christians will inevitably turn to II Peter. It is there we find the claim that the Bible was written by holy men of God—"holy men of God spake as they were moved by the Holy Ghost." (II Peter 1:21). However, a number of confusing questions and contradictions are presented in the book. To begin, in this same passage we find the author exhorting his fellow Christians to have faith in the parousia—the coming of the Lord. And he is not referencing the Old Testament to support that prophecy. The author is claiming that he, James, and John heard the voice of God confirm the promise at the transfiguration of Jesus (v. 17-18). The problem this presents is that the author could not be Peter because the general belief in the parousia didn't become problematic until after Peter's death.

Georg Kummel, *Introduction to the New Testament*, presents the arguments that make it obvious to all critical scholars that II Peter is a pseudepigraph. While the author defends the parousia, we find evidence that he was already introducing the shift from an imminent expectation to a future hope; a doctrinal error that wasn't recognized until the second century.

II Peter is an expanded version of the Epistle of Jude. Both open with very similar greetings. Both are addressed to the believers who are allegedly saved through God and Jesus Christ. Both begin urging their readers to be diligent in the faith, and both warn of ungodly men who would corrupt the truth. Like the Gospels, one copies freely from the other.

With the exception of the additional verses in II Peter, both passages follow the same outline and use almost the exact same phraseology—emphasized here with italics. Beginning in the second chapter, II Peter addresses the same subjects as Jude: (1) They speak of ungodly men and false prophets who will bring in heresies, even *denying the Lord*. (2) They refer to the angels that sinned who were cast into hell and delivered unto *chains of darkness unto judgment*. (3) They list examples of God's wrath upon the wicked and salvation for the believers. II Peter notes Noah's deliverance from the flood, the condemnation of Sodom and Gomorrah, and the deliverance of Lot. Jude speaks of God saving his people out of Egypt and then destroying the unbelievers, and also uses Sodom and Gomorrah as an example. (4) Both speak of fornicators *going after strange flesh*, or *walk after the flesh*, and who *speak evil of dignitaries*. (5) Still alluding to the wicked, Jude says that even the archangel Michael, when contending with the Devil, dared not bring *railing accusations* against him. II Peter softens the claim by changing Michael to angels and bringing the *railing accusations* against *them*—the wicked in question. (6) Both call the wicked *brute beasts*. Both accuse the people of following after *Balaam*. Both refer to them as *wells without water* and *clouds carried about of winds*.

When we consider that II Peter is nothing more than an expanded version of Jude, and understand that the author's condemnation of the ungodly isn't limited to the then present dissidents, but was projected into a future parousia, it becomes obvious that the work was written to counteract the accusations of the Gnostics, and present an explanation for Jesus' delayed return. Therefore, it is almost universally recognized that II Peter was written after Jude and not the reverse.

Additional information that denies Peter as the author is the fact that he was a Jew and the work smacks of Hellenism. From Georg Kummel's *Introduction to the New Testament*, pp. 430-4:

> 2. The conceptual world and the rhetorical language are so strongly influenced by Hellenism as to rule out Peter definitely, nor could it have been written by one of his helpers or pupils under instructions from Peter. Not even at some time after the death of the apostle....

3. The letter has a keen interest in opposing the denial of the Christians' expectation of the parousia. 1:12 ff already deals with the hope of the parousia, which is based on the fact of the transfiguration of Jesus and the OT prophecy. In 3:3 ff there is a direct polemic against those who deny the parousia. These ask scornfully, "Where is the promise of the parousia of Christ?" and draw attention to the fact that since the fathers have fallen asleep everything remains as it has been from the beginning of creation (3:4). In I Clem 23:3 f and II Clem 11:2 ff too, there is adduced a writing which was obviously read in Christian circles, in which is laid down the challenge "We have already heard that in the days of our fathers, but look, we are become old and nothing of that has happened to us." I Clem was written ca. 95, and II Clem can hardly have been written earlier than 150. We have, therefore, historical evidence from the end of the first century onward for the disdainful skepticism which is expressed in II Pet 3:3 ff. But it is the Gnostics of the second century who have opposed the parousia and reinterpreted it along spiritualistic lines....

4. Also indicative of the second century is the appeal to a collection of Pauline letters from which "statements that are hard to understand" have been misinterpreted by the false teachers, and to further normative writings which include not only the OT but also the developing NT (3:16). In view of the difficulty in understanding "scripture," and its ambiguity, II Pet offers the thesis that "no prophetic scripture allows an individual interpretation" because men have spoken under the power of the Holy Spirit (1:20 f). Since not every Christian has the Spirit, the explanation of Scripture is reserved for the ecclesiastical teaching office. Accordingly we find ourselves without doubt far beyond the time of Peter and into the epoch of "early Catholicism."

It is certain, therefore, that II Pet does not originate with Peter, and this is today widely acknowledged. This point of view can be confirmed through two further facts.

5. As in the case of the Pastorals, the pseudonymity in II Pet is carried through consistently by means of heavy stress on the Petrine authorship (see above, p. 430). The author adduces his authority not only on the basis of the fiction of a "testament of Peter" but also by reference back to I Pet in 3:1 f, intending II Pet only to "recall" (1:12, 15; 3:1 f) what was said in I Pet to the extent that it corresponds to the interpretation which the author of II Pet

wants to give to I Pet. This appeal to the apostolic authority of Peter and his letter is obviously occasioned by the sharpening of the Gnostic false teaching which is being combated in Jude, as a result of a consistent denial of the parousia of the false teachers. In this way, the apostle has become the "guarantor of the tradition" (1:12 f), and as a consequence of the abandonment of the near expectation (3:8) the parousia is stripped of its christological character and functions as an anthropologically oriented doctrine of rewards. In its consistent quality the pseudonymity betrays the late origins of II Pet.

6. In spite of its heavy stress on Petrine authorship, II Pet is nowhere mentioned in the second century. The apologists, Irenaeus, Tertullian, Cyprian, Clement of Alexandria, and the Muratorian Canon are completely silent about it. Its first attestation is in Origen, but according to him the letter is contested. Eusebius lists it among the antilegomena. . . Even down to the fourth century II Pet was largely unknown or not recognized as canonical.

In Acts chapter two we find Peter cursing Ananias and Sapphira with death because they (indirectly) denied the immanency of the parousia. Yet, we are suppose to believe that years later, when the event tarries, Peter begins teaching it as a future event.

It should be obvious that the Christians were having trouble explaining the lengthening duration of an event that was suppose to occur at any moment, and that II Peter was written in an attempt to combat the denials of the skeptics. So, when we find that the book to which Christians turn in support of the Bible is a forgery, what does that say concerning the entire "Word of God"?

THE INCONGRUITY OF CHRISTIAN BELIEFS

Just what is it that God does?

A number of my Christian friends and relatives are concerned for my immortal soul; so much so they strive for that unique testimony or biblical phrase that will lift the scales from my eyes. Their burden is so great I cannot help but feel empathy for their anguish as they assure me that God is not through with me, that he will yet reveal himself to me, and other such verbiage. And as they struggle with their raw emotions I wonder at the incongruity of the situation.

They all assure me that an all-powerful God has a plan or purpose for me, that he has sent them to assure me that he will *reveal* himself to me. They may even go so far as to declare themselves God's prophet. Why then are they so sad? If they are so sure this good thing is going to happen, why are they burdened? Should they not deliver this prophecy with joy and happiness?

Other thoughts invade my mind: If God is so powerful, why does he need witnesses? If he wants everyone to be saved (Jn. 3-17)—come to know him, acknowledge him as God—why doesn't he just reveal himself to everyone? Why has the world been split asunder by the questions: Does God exist? Does Jesus exist? Which is the right Church? Is the Bible divine? Is Judaism, Christianity, or Islam the true religion? Why is the Bible so vague, contradictory, and ambiguous? Surely, if there were a god who wanted everyone to believe in his existence—an all-powerful god with unlimited resources who could do anything—he could create a promotional plan that was easily comprehensible. A plan that presented a clear, believable story; one that proved his existence, stated the terms, requirements, and rewards for acceptance as plainly as a humanly conceived contract. Instead, the question is not about whether one chooses to follow God, but whether there IS a God.

We are assured this is a loving god. One who "loves the little children." Who blesses those who serve him. However, a careful and unbiased reading of the Old Testament reveals a cruel, vengeful god who *chooses* a special people and slaughters everyone else at will, including those "little children." A god who is vacillating and indecisive, an angry god who cannot control his temper. A god who had to be corrected and advised by Moses. A god who allowed the Catholic Church to select and compile the New Testament, and to create a hideous modus operandi that condoned the same vicious and inhumane practices of the Old Testament; a dictating power that exhibited hatred for those who disagreed, and imposed ostracization, torture, and death for non-conformist. And then this God did the same thing with Islam.

This same god has stood idle for over 1700 years while three separate groups of fanatics have used his name to run amok throughout the world, waging war, devastating economies and countries, and slaughtering millions of people.

My Christian friends are able to cover all this atrocious history with faith, and expect me to look forward with great expectations of joy that this savior has a plan for me. Instead, I shutter with horror that their prophecies might come to pass. And I wonder, if perhaps those tears in my friends' eyes aren't justified.

If you've sensed bitterness in my words you may be wondering, "How can this man profess friendship with Christians?" It is simple, where they believe me to be misinformed and mislead, I believe they allow faith to override reason and common sense. It is not a matter of dislike, but mutual pity.

During the Dark Ages the Catholic Church's power was absolute; no one could work or own property unless they followed the Church's dictates; criticism brought quick and sever reprises. Few people could read so all the power was in the clergy. During this time, the Church implanted outrageous, mythical tales within the superstitious minds of an ignorant and suppressed people—a people who were forced to vow allegiance to a wicked and despotic regime. Chief among those tales was that of a resurrected Jesus and the promise of a heavenly reward, drawn from the mythical tale related in the gospels of Matthew, Mark, Luke, and John. For fifteen hundred years this tale was the only hope for a suppressed and brainwashed populace. Imagine how hard it would be to question a dream of escape, a purpose for living, a glimpse of heaven that had been reiterated and passed down from your parents, grandparents, and great-grandparents—for generations—a story everyone believed? So how could they possible know that their holy book was a jumble of lies, contradictions, and interpolations? That indoctrination was so successful that even today the average Christian will not read the Bible with the intent of finding truth. The story of Jesus presented to every prospective convert is a Bible unto itself. You can show a Christian specific, clear, contradictory Scripture—Scripture they cannot refute and they'll turn to faith to excuse their ignorance. Why? Because underneath that exterior of love, dedication, and concern for others is fear. Tell a Christian that there is no god who holds sway in the matters of men and you can see the fear in his eyes—they might even flicker momentarily upward. Why? Sanctions. The punishment for sins. The loss of heaven. A fiery, burning hell instead. Religions are perpetrated upon fear: punishment for sin, the lost of reward.

There is no basis for such fear, and the proof is easily discernible within the New Testament. While the real story of Jesus is not evident, there is ample proof within the New Testament, within historical and archaeological research, scientific evidence, and common sense to disproof the fables of virgin births, resurrections from the dead, and the other miracles numerated within Church teachings.

If this proof is so readily available, you might ask, why hasn't it already been revealed? That is a good question, and one I can't answer definitively. I can only guess—faith. Christians still don't want to admit that the story of heaven is a fable. Every time I reach a point of contention with a Christian where they cannot refute reason, they turn to faith and began speaking of "feelings," and "miracles" they've experienced. In a world where tales of mental incompetence and delusional experiences are well documented facts recorded in medical journals, proven in practice, and frequently aired on television Christians still refuse to accept facts over faith.

I don't view Christians or any other religious adherents as evil or as adversaries. When I observe the lives of Christians I see caring, honest people who love their children and are an asset to their community. I believe there is a relationship between these values and the Christian moral values that they chose to embrace rather than the evil values imposed by the early Catholic Church and those exhibited today by Islamic extremists.

What most Christians, and adherents of other religions, cannot comprehend is that all their accomplishments come from within themselves—not from a god. There are numerous verses in the New Testament that state such: Matt. 9:21-22, 11:23, 13:58, 14:31, and 17:20.

One of the first things that struck me as incongruous about Christian beliefs was the fact that their god is described as being all-powerful, omniscient, a mover and shaker, the center of every facet of being, the creator of everything—every atom, every philosophy. And yet, he does nothing. Yes, believers *give* him *credit* for every imagined good they might perceive while denying his authorship of such catastrophes as natural disasters, diseases, and wars. Even though he claims to "... make peace, and create evil..." (Is. 45:7), Christians are quick to attribute all evil to the depravity of humans—or some indeterminate creature. For some unfathomable reason, God is helpless to intervene. For some inexplicable reason, He chooses to unleash storms, wildfires, earthquakes and epidemics upon his creation, or create numerous, contending sects and allow them to slaughter each other in religious wars.

Did God not assured Abraham that he would give him the promised land for an eternal inheritance. Did he not preserve and bless Abraham's first son, Ishmael, and make him the progenitor of all twenty-two nations in today's Arab League? Did Jesus, a Jew, not die that his father might introduce Christianity?

No, God did not "invent" all those false religions—Judaism, Christianity, Islam—man did.

So, what does God do? Nothing. *Bad things*, that cannot be attributed to evil men, such as natural disasters are grudging admitted to being random because, of course, God wouldn't afflict the innocent children, would he? No? Have you ever read the Old Testament—really read it?

Take a moment to contemplate all the changes that are occurring in our world: the wars, over-population, global warming, natural disasters, all the *bad things*. Now consider the good, or what might be considered good: advancements in medicines, economic booms, technological and industrial advancements. Tell me, what is the common denominator? Man. Man, by his destruction of our environment, might even be held liable, to some degree, for the natural disasters. Can it not be seen that without man none of these changes would have occurred?

There is no proven incident of God ever doing anything. There are probably billions of daily incidents where believers—in all three religions—*see* God's interventions, but they are only perceived, not actual. God has never replaced a lost arm or leg, men have. God has never restored a person's vision, optometry is a common human occupation. God has never polluted a river, men do so without even trying. Every accomplishment, good or bad, may be attributed to man, but we have no verifiable record of God ever doing anything.

Today, there are only four major religions that worship a god: Hinduism, which recognizes a panoply of gods, Judaism, Christianity, and Islam. The last three worship the same god. If you fall into one of these groups you should question your teachings, as the writer of I Th. 5:21 says, "Prove all things: hold fast that which is good." And not, as one dear Christian replied to me, "I have proved it, through the miracles and wonders God has worked in my life." That is not proof, that is speculative, unfounded, delusional thinking.

There have been many well know and *powerful* gods that reigned for thousands of years within numerous cultures, much like the triune Christian god. No doubt they *answered* prayers just as Jesus, Jehovah, and/or Allah does today. Records recount incidents of miracles, trances, feelings, prophecies, and speaking in tongues—just as adherents of our present day god, or gods, do. But, where are they? Gone. When their believers ceased to believe, they vanished. Why? Because they were no gods at all, only the futile imaginings of men. Ask yourself, what would happen to Jesus—or Yahwah or Allah—if everyone stopped believing? He could do nothing. Men's faith in *him*—whichever *him* that might be—would be recognized as their own strength, and, most certainly, the hatred and atrocities that have existed between these three warring factions would cease.

Isn't it time we stopped believing in fairy tales?

IN SEARCH OF THE CHRISTIAN GOD

Contradiction, falsehood, and confusion: is it any wonder that
believers are spiritualizing the Bible?

According to the *World Christian Encyclopedia* there are
nineteen major world religions which may be divided into
two hundred and seventy smaller aggregations. Within
one of those worldwide aggregations, Christianity, over thirty-four
thousand groups have been counted. Unless we conclude that the
Christian god sanctioned different divine doctrines it is evident
that only one group has true communion with their master and is
able to properly interpret their Bible. Otherwise, one must admit
that communication with God is a very nebulous and questionable
endeavor. If only one group is in God's will, that puts the odds of
choosing the *right* group at over thirty-four thousand to one. Is there
any wonder there is confusion, animosities, and hostilities? So many
denominations, so many doctrines, so much mystification—how
can the average person understand?

When we turn to the ministers of all this confusion the advice
most often rendered is to just believe and trust to the guidance of
the Holy Spirit, or something to that extent. The inference being that
by surrendering one's own reasoning ability and allowing the Spirit
to lead, the confused new convert will be guided into all of God's
truth. The fallacy of this reasoning is evidenced by the multiplicity of
different Christian groups.

Obviously, we have, not one, but thousands of Christian churches:
from the extreme fundamentalist to the libertarians who welcome
the belief in other gods, or those who profess no god at all. From

the literalist to the allegorist, from the pacifist to the activist, from those who believe in a sprinkling baptism to those who insist upon total immersion. From those who teach one work of grace to those who teach two, or three, there are endless combinations. Still, there are believers who will shrug their shoulders and say, "There are only personal differences, none of which contradict the core principles of God's Word." Why then, do we find fundamentalist groups who refuse to acknowledge Catholics, Mormons, Jehovah Witnesses, and other denominations as Christians and declare them the servants of Satan? And, why do the Catholics claim there is no salvation outside the Catholic Church? If any groups are denounced as false Christians, then such actions deny the unity of principles, which obviously makes one's denominational choice a soul threatening difference.

This lack of unity creates major problems. Imagine, perhaps a million ministers from those thirty-four thousand groups stepping into pulpits around the world on Sunday (or Saturday) morning. How would they define a major tenet of belief such as the prerequisites for personal salvation? What makes a Christian? The Catholic Church, the compiler of the New Testament and originator of most of the generally accepted doctrines, has obviously given the subject much consideration. From the *Original Catholic Encyclopedia*, under the topic *Salvation*:

> The Council of Trent describes the process of salvation from sin in the case of an adult with great minuteness (Sess. VI, v-vi).

> It begins with the grace of God which touches a sinner's heart, and calls him to repentance. This grace cannot be merited; it proceeds solely from the love and mercy of God. Man may receive or reject this inspiration of God, he may turn to God or remain in sin. Grace does not constrain man's free will.

> Thus assisted the sinner is disposed for salvation from sin; he believes in the revelation and promises of God, he fears God's justice, hopes in his mercy, trusts that God will be merciful to him for Christ's sake, begins to love God as the source of all justice, hates and detests his sins.

> This disposition is followed by justification itself, which consists not in the mere remission of sins, but in the sanctification and

renewal of the inner man by the voluntary reception of God's grace and gifts, whence a man becomes just instead of unjust, a friend instead of a foe and so an heir according to hope of eternal life. This change happens either by reason of a perfect act of charity elicited by a well disposed sinner or by virtue of the Sacrament either of Baptism or of Penance according to the condition of the respective subject laden with sin. The Council further indicates the causes of this change. By the merit of the Most Holy Passion through the Holy Spirit, the charity of God is shed abroad in the hearts of those who are justified.

Against the heretical tenets of various times and sects we must hold

- that the initial grace is truly gratuitous and supernatural;
- that the human will remains free under the influence of this grace;
- that man really cooperates in his personal salvation from sin;
- that by justification man is really made just, and not merely declared or reputed so;
- that justification and sanctification are only two aspects of the same thing, and not ontologically and chronologically distinct realities;
- that justification excludes all moral sin from the soul, so that the just man is no way liable to the sentence of death at God's judgment-seat.
  https://www.ecatholic2000.com/cathopedia/vol13/volthirteen365.shtml

As stated, the process is indeed described with "great minuteness." On the other hand, many Christian denominations quote Jesus' instruction to Nicodemus in John 3:15: That whosoever believeth in him should not perish, but have eternal life, and insist that salvation requires only a belief. Many fundamentalist contend that such a belief must be exhibited by a sinless life, while some Baptist cry, "Once saved, always save." To the extreme, there are those who declare that all will be saved. If there is so much dissension in regard to the most basic tenet of belief, how can there be any less confusion about the lesser doctrines?

The source of contention is evident—Christians simply don't understand their own Bible. I've actually heard Christians admit as much and thank God because they don't have to concern themselves.

They defer to the ancient Church fathers and rest their hope in this life and eternal life, upon the teachings of those unknown men. In contrast, many Christians will shutter at the idea of deferring to the opinion of the ancients. Then how did they come to the knowledge of Jesus' saving grace? Who wrote the books of their New Testament? Who selected those books? How do they know of Jesus—of God? In every case, they are depending upon the oft-repeated words of some ancient, unknown human.

I've had Christians freely admit that they can't understand the Bible, but immediately assure me that they don't have to, because Reverend Roberts, or Brother Wilson, can really explain it. Here we have a double oxymoron. First, if they can't understand, how do they know their revered teacher is delivering a proper explanation? Secondly, if the teacher does do such a great job why don't the listeners understand? This same thought may be applied to the Christian who defers to the wisdom of the Church's founding fathers—if he doesn't understand, how does he know he's receiving the truth?

But such ignorance isn't limited to those who choose not to study the Bible. Another type of ignorance infects many learned doctors of divinity, professors of religious philosophy, and spirit filled evangelicals. It is an ignorance that found its roots in the suppressive rule of early Catholicism. It is the type of ignorance Jesus warned against in Luke:

> He is like a man which built an house, and digged deep, and laid the foundation on a rock: and when the flood arose, the stream beat vehemently upon that house, and could not shake it: for it was founded upon a rock. But he that heareth, and doeth not, is like a man that without a foundation built an house upon the earth; against which the stream did beat vehemently, and immediately it fell; and the ruin of that house was great (Luke 6:48&49).

Although this passage alludes to a belief in Jesus Christ as a foundation for personal salvation the same principle may be applied to Church doctrine, Church history, Scripture, or an argument based on any of the aforementioned. A strong argument must be built upon facts, not assertions. The ignorance of the intellectual is in pursuing an argument based upon faith. By faith—God is. By faith—the worlds were formed. By faith—Jesus died for man. By faith—

that same Jesus rose from the grave. But when we ask how one can even be sure God exists, Christians quickly point to the universe about us. They note the complexity of our own bodies, the infinity of space, or the impossibility of a watch evolving—and declare God. Nevertheless, since such evidence only indicates, at best, a creative force, how are we to know that force is God? Here our teachers turn to the Bible. We are told Paul declared that God "made heaven, and earth, and the sea, and all things that are therein." And of course the full creation story is affirmed in the book of Genesis. Their reasoning isn't just illogical, it's confusing. First, we're expected to believe in a god we can't see, hear, or touch—a god incapable of communicating with man. Then we're told he does communicate. He communicates with man via the Holy Spirit. That he dwells within the heart of each believer and personally directs their life. And how is that working? I believe we've found an explanation for the thirty-four thousand different Christian groups. Next, we're told he gave us the Bible—written by holy prophets. How do we know this? Perhaps those prophets simply made it all up. Wait a minute. Let me see if I get this. Man can't prove his God exists, but he has a book written by God that proves his existence? Doesn't that strain your sense of credibility just a bit? If I told you this article is an excerpt from a book on Christian history I'd just written would that make it any more credible—of course not. Neither can you use a humanly created story to prove the existence of a divine being.

The New Testament tells us Jesus died for man's salvation and that Jesus was raised from the grave for man's justification. All this is sure and without doubt—if you have faith in the Bible. But who has ever proven the Bible? Faith is the strongest basis possible for a Christian, or for a believer of any religion, but it is nothing more than hearsay evidence in a world of facts. To unravel all this confusion we must define and dissect two religious concepts as taught by Christianity. Those concepts are *faith* and *truth*.

Both faith and truth have what I term a standard and a religious definition. That standard definition for faith, according to the Merriam-Webster Dictionary is: "…complete confidence in someone or something." The religious interpretation has come to mean *belief in God.*

The definition for truth is described similarly. Again from Merriam-Webster: "… that which conforms to fact or reality." The

American Standard's definition is almost identical: "1. Conformity to fact or actuality. 2. A statement proven to be or accepted as true." And in defining the word truth in relation to God: "*Christian Science: a synonym for God.*" Yet God has never been *factually* proven to *actually* exist. In both cases Christianity, and other religions, have effectively invented their own definition of both words.

Almost everyone over the age of majority knows that truth means the opposite of false or a lie. Even those simple little true and false tests administer in elementary schools prove that young children understand the basic meaning of the word. The discerning of truth is a science. It can be tested and proven. But religions have made a mockery of the word by creating their own definition, a term best described as religious truth or Christian Science. Where truth, in actuality, deals with facts—such as in a court of law in which evidence is presented to prove a statement or deed. Religious fables cannot be proven beyond assertions based solely on faith. Today, theologians and fervent believers boldly declare *The Truth*, and are even insulted when it is questioned. Without a shred of evidence, with straight faces and passion in their voices, they tell stories of virgin births and resurrections from the dead, and demand that all believe in a god whose existence cannot be proven.

But what is this *truth* that Christians view as the final authority? It isn't just the Bible, or the Word. It infers a much broader meaning that includes not only the written word, but the doctrines, precepts, and values that have come to identify Christianity. In effect the two have become synonymous, Christianity is truth; all contradictory religions, doctrines, or philosophies are false. Christianity has the truth— Christianity is truth.

Since this supposition can't be proven, how then, can intelligent, educated, and often brilliant people believe so strongly in unfounded and unsupportable assertions? It is all a matter of using faith to define truth.

The power of religions is not derived from an invisible, ever-present, supernatural being that hovers watchfully beyond the stars—it is derived from *belief* in such a deity. Such faith empowers believers to "move mountains" or "raise the dead". The principle is best summed up in a seventies self-help guru's credo: "Whatever man can believe, man can achieve."

To illustrate, imagine someone shooting a basketball from mid-court. If the shooter persists long enough he will eventually make a shot, and as long as he can believe he will keep shooting. If he becomes exhausted, he will rest and resume shooting—if he can still believe. If he lacks the strength to toss the ball the distance he'll practice until he is strong enough—if he can believe. Such a goal is possible as long as the shooter maintains his faith. If he becomes discouraged and quits, the faith is gone and the endeavor becomes impossible. So long as the shooter believes, the task is possible. When he doubts, the task is doomed.

Faith is one of the most powerful driving forces common to human beings. Look at the world man has built simply because he had faith. We enjoy all the bounties of our great country because Columbus had faith in a theory that the earth was round. We enjoy our democratic freedom because our founding fathers had faith in the idea of a government by the people. We have prospered through industrial and technological advancements because someone had faith that machines could be built or scientific principles could be applied. For those who might respond that all these accomplishments were achieved because the United States has been blessed by God, I will suggest that they study the history of the Church during the Dark Ages. There they will discover the genuine results of an all-powerful theocracy in action.

A prime example of faith in action may be found in the civil rights movement ignited by Dr. Martin Luther King Jr. No doubt, Reverend King's faith was in his god, but the movement succeeded because of faith in Reverend King's dream. The proof is the fact that today there is probably a Martin Luther King Jr. street in every major U.S. city; where it would be hard to find one named Jehovah Blvd. or God Almighty Avenue. Other evidence that faith is the power, not a divine being, may be found in the rhetoric of leaders such as Adolph Hitler and Mussolini, who united the masses of Europe in an effort to establish a Third Reich. In each case, the power was faith. Doctor King, Hitler, and Mussolini were only the figureheads. When that power is accredited to religious faith, then faith becomes the believers' god.

There are a number of New Testament passages that show the power comes from the human psychic, not a divine being. For example, in Matthew 9:20-22, a woman believed she would be healed if she touched Jesus' garment. Notice, the belief was based upon touching his garment—not that he would heal her. Had her faith been solely in Jesus she would have only had to believe. Touching the garment was only the focal point. It was a labor she appointed herself, an act she could perform that would prove her faith. Jesus' reply was, "...thy faith hath made thee whole."

Another example is found in Matthew 14:22-31. The disciples were in a boat on a storm tossed sea and Jesus came to them walking upon the water. (Whoever wrote this had, obviously, never been on a storm tossed sea where the surface might rise or fall thirty to sixty feet in an instant.) Peter, desiring to go to Jesus, began walking on the water also but became fearful and began to sink. After Jesus rescued him, he rebuked Peter by saying, "O thou of little faith, wherefore didst thou doubt?" Indicating, once again, that the power is in the believer—not the god.

In Matthew 17:14-20 we find Jesus' disciples were unable to cast out a devil because of their unbelief. Which were they unable to believe, their ability, or the power of Jesus? You might choose either answer. Whether they doubted their ability or that of Jesus the failure was the lack of faith.

But what of those impossible miracles mentioned in the Bible? If one believes them, are they possible? How about walking on water? If one truly believes he can walk upon water, is it possible? The point is not whether one can walk (unaided) upon water, but whether one can *believe*. Do you believe you can walk on water? Since you have probably tried it at least once in your lifetime, the answer is most likely, no.

Another point to consider is the ministries of faith healers such as Oral Roberts, A. A. Allen, Ernest Angley, or Pat Robertson. Why are such healers able to cure invisible and therefore questionable ailments, such as arthritis, gall stones, or cancer—but never replace missing physical parts such as eyes or limbs? Why have we never seen an amputee grow a new arm or leg on national TV? And why has no one ever restored life to an embalmed corpse? Because there are simply some things that are scientifically impossible and no amount of faith can change scientific facts.

I'm mindful of a joke I once hear of a Christian who had fallen over a cliff and was hanging tenaciously to a cracking and weakening root. He prayed to his god for deliverance, all the while assuring his deity of his trust and devotion. Then a voice from above instructed: "Let go." Was it the voice of his god, or perhaps someone just out of sight? If the fellow truly believed and did turn loose, would he fall? Could he maintain his belief all the way down? Personally, I doubt it. On the other hand, there are stories of such survivors, broken and shattered, praising god's wondrous delivering power from their hospital beds. Other questions then arise: Was their deliverance really affected by divine intervention? If so: why were they in the hospital? Where was the miracle? Would it not appear that gravity prevailed rather than god?

Why do you suppose faith is the unquestionable, undeniable, prerequisite of all religions? Why do all gods demand it? Why are all gods invisible and unknowable? Why is it impossible to scientifically, or even logically, prove the existence of a god? And why do they disappear when faith vanishes? In Matthew 13:58 we find that Jesus was unable to perform miracles in his own country because the people knew him and had no faith in his claims. The power is within the believer, and the healer or miracle worker only has to stoke that fire.

Consider the Christian religion. When the proselyte accepts God, is his belief based upon the word of God or the disciple who conveyed the story? That is, who spoke to him—who told him the story? Obviously it wasn't God personally otherwise there would be no need for preachers.

Ultimately then, the believer's faith is based upon man—not a god. The importance of that faith is made evident by the extreme measures taken by the Catholic Church during the Dark Ages when their theocratic government reigned supreme. To protect *the faith* they either enslaved the minds of men or destroyed their bodies, all for the glory of their god. Why? If the power was with their god why didn't he preserve his church? Why was it necessary that the Church revert to military conquests, human deprivations, torture, and genocide to preserve *the faith*?

What happens when faith fails, when prayers are unanswered or the minister is unable to perform? Such failures automatically fall upon the believer because god is perfect and beyond fault, therefore the believer obviously lost faith. Such reasoning preserves the integrity of the god.

Also, it is very convenient that gods demand belief by faith only. Why? Because to question or reason negates faith, and without faith religions melt away like an early morning fog before the sun. Without faith, religious truths stand alone in the sunlight exposed for what they are, empty, useless, fables.

For Christianity to survive it has openly promoted a triune godhead: the Father, Son, and Holy Spirit. Behind the scenes, it has spawned upon its unsuspecting adherents a shadow godhead that has enslaved the minds of its followers. That trinity is the Church (God), Truth (the Word or Jesus), and Faith (the Spirit). The Church is the visible head of power. It claims authority to chose and interpret the words of its God, to force those words on all mankind, and punish dissidents. Truth is the Bible and its doctrines, which the Church compiled and legislated to empower itself. Faith is the power it uses to inflame the emotions and cloud the reason of its adherents.

Faith is the god of religions. When faith fails, the god disappears because he can't even exist without the strength of his followers. Jesus is nothing without the people, the churches, the wealth, and power. What do you suppose would happen to him if all Christians stopped believing? Would he not join the ranks of the once powerful, but now debunked, deities of the past? Consider all the gods of the ancient Egyptians, Persians, Greeks, or Romans—mighty nations with powerful gods. What happened to Zeus, Isis, Mithras, and the pantheon of hundreds of gods when their followers lost faith? Where are they today? Do you suppose they are still roaming the deserts of North Africa? Or are they sitting on Mount Olympus, plotting the overthrow of Yahweh and Allah? Ah, but you say: "They were no gods at all; only the vain imaginings of man." To which I reply— precisely my point. There are no gods at all.

Religions are evolutionary concepts. The first known god was, in actuality, not a god, but a goddess. The concept of a divine being was initially bestowed upon women because of their mysterious ability to give birth. They were revered and worshiped as the mother of life. Then, apparently men became aware of the role they played in procreation and soon the mother figure evolved into the powerful, jealous, avenging, male god; to wit, the blood-thirsty Yahweh of the Hebrews. But the cruel, vengeful, Hebrew god did not fit the Christians' merciful, self-sacrificing and forgiving Jesus; so, once again, man's concept of god underwent a metamorphosis. No doubt, sometime in the probably not too distant future, social knowledge will outgrow the ignorance and superstitions of the Jesus myths. The believers will transfer their faith to a new deity, a new religion will be born, and the name of Jesus will pass into the annals of mythology along with all the other ancient gods who have lost their followers.

FAITH AND REASON

Christianity has become so ingrained within our society, has
become so adept at presenting an image of righteousness,
until that image is often associated with right thinking,
knowledgeable, truth. But it was not always so.

As a young man, I worked at a photographic studio where they
hired a young man who still believed in Santa Claus. Charles
was about eighteen, and it was probably his first real job. He'd
been working with us a couple of years before we discovered his
strange belief.

One day he was talking with me and a couple of other guys, and
somehow the subject arose. At first, we thought he was kidding us,
but as he talked, our perception began to change.

"I write a letter to Santa every year, and get just what I ask for,"
he assured us.

"Come on!" a guy named Vic exclaimed. "You trying to tell us
you don't know your Dad is Santa Claus ... that he's the one putting
out the toys?" Vic was only a few years older than Charles.

"I stopped asking for toys years ago." Charles said with a touch
of indignation.

"Whatever!"

"And my father died when I was seven," Charles added.

We exchanged looks, no doubt, each wondering if this guy was
pulling our leg. If so, he was good. "These letters," I said, "I guess you
mail them to the North Pole, right?"

"No, I give them to my mother."

I'm not a poker player, but even so, I'd never play poker with
this guy.

"Ha!" Webb, the fourth member of the group jeered. "Nobody
can be this dumb. You gotta know it's your mother."

"No, it's Santa," Charles insisted. "My mother only mails the letters."

"Let'm guess," a grin split Webb's face, "Your mother's got the address?"

"The address?"

"Come on!" Webb exploded. "Knock it off. You can't be that stupid."

"Oh, I get it." Charles said. "No, my mother has nothing to do with it."

"How do you know?" Vic jumped back into the fray.

"Cause I get things she could never give me."

"Like what?" Vic asked.

"Well, when I was sixteen, I asked for a car and my Uncle Ted gave me an '89 Civic. Of course, that was on the 27th of December, and not actually from Santa, but I think Santa uses people sometimes."

"Santa uses people …" Webb repeated. "Come on, numb-skull, it was a coincident."

"No," Charles insisted. "Can't you see? I'm getting older, moving away from home. I even have my own place now. So, Santa can't just come down the chimney and bring my gifts."

"Come down the chimney …" Webb left the remark hanging.

"Metaphorically speaking."

"Med a for—" Webb was interrupted.

"Look, I can prove it. Year before last, I asked for a good job and I was hired here. Last year, I asked for a raise and got a two dollar raise right along with my Christmas bonus. Don't you see—right at Christmas?"

⸙

Of course, there was no Charles, no Vic or Webb, but I did work at a photographic studio. Tell me though. Did you believe the story? Did you wonder … perhaps, just a bit? But is this tale really all that incredulous? Not really, millions of people believed that Saint Nickolas gave bags of gold to a poor man with three daughters. This was back in the fourth century. Nickolas was just a rich man then. In those days a young woman's father had to offer prospective husbands something of value—a dowry. The larger the dowry, the better the chance that a young woman would find a good husband. Without a dowry, a woman was likely to be sold into prostitution. Mysteriously, on three different occasions, a bag of gold appeared in their home, providing the needed dowries. And everyone knew Saint Nickolas had to have been the giver.

The reason he is known as Santa Claus is because he became the protector of children. On one occasion,three theological students were traveling on their way to study in Athens. A wicked innkeeper robbed and murdered them, hiding their remains in a large pickling tub. It so happened that Bishop Nicholas, traveling along the same route, stopped at this very inn. In the night he dreamed of the crime, got up, and summoned the innkeeper. As Nicholas prayed earnestly to God the three boys were restored to life and wholeness.

In France the story is told of three small children, wandering in their play until lost, lured, and captured by an evil butcher. St. Nicholas appears and appeals to God to return them to life and to their families. So, St. Nicholas is the patron and protector of children.

One of the oldest stories showing St. Nicholas as a protector of children takes place long after his death. The townspeople of Myra were celebrating the good saint on the eve of his feast day when a band of Arab pirates from Crete came into the district. As they were leaving town, they snatched a young boy, Basilios, to make into a slave. The emir, or ruler, selected Basilios to be his personal cup-bearer. For the next year, Basilios waited on the king, bringing his wine in a beautiful golden cup. At the next St. Nicholas' feast day, St. Nicholas suddenly whisked Basilios up and away, and set him down at his home back in Myra—still holding the king's golden cup.

Does anyone today believe these tales? Perhaps, perhaps not, but centuries ago they were believed by millions. And don't forget, the Catholic Church made him a saint. "Yes," you might say, "hundreds of years ago, when people were ignorance and would believe anything. To that, I must agree, and add—back when the stories of Jesus were created. But today? Not much has changed, the Church is still making saints—and Christians are still believing fairytales.

If you're a Christian you might exclaim, "Surely, two billion people can't be wrong."

⋄⊰✻⊱⋄

Today, when Christians are stripped of every reasonable argument to defend their beliefs, they turn to faith. Why is this necessary? Because Christians cannot support their beliefs with rational arguments. It's easy to prove God is not omniscient when we're told the earth is only six thousand years old; or that he isn't omnibenevolent when Amos asks, "Does evil befall a city unless the Lord has done it?" Their argument implodes when they then try to explain that God's ways are far above us and he is thus unknowable—their answer has just given us two attributes that deny their assertion.

This is where they will turn to faith, insisting that we must believe and trust the Holy Spirit to lead us into all understanding. At this point, the debate ends. They have entered the inner sanctum of their spiritual realm and never hear when they'd asked if it matters which one of the 3400 Christian groups the Holy Spirit might lead us into.

There are thousands of other gods that people worship today. Most likely, Christians rejected these other gods without ever looking into their religions, or checking out their books. They simply accepted the god of their family or society. Stephen F. Roberts, B.A. and M.Litt, mid-nineteenth century historian, summed it up rather nicely:

> I contend that we are both atheists. I just believe in one less god than you do. When you understand why you dismiss all the other possible gods, you will understand why I dismiss yours.

A rational person rejects all human gods equally, because all are equally imaginary. How do we know that they are imaginary? If one of these thousands of gods were actually real, then his followers would be experiencing real, undeniable benefits. These benefits would be obvious to everyone. The followers of a true god would pray, and their prayers would be answered. The followers of a true god would therefore live longer, have fewer diseases, have lots more money, etc. There would be thousands of statistical markers surrounding the followers of a true god.

I can already hear the Christian's response: "God has blessed me, blessed his Church. I have a loving family, blessed with good health, a beautiful home, and the fellowship of hundreds of brothers and sisters."

Can the Jews, Hindus, Muslims, and followers of Budda not make similar claims? And what of the "prosperity ministers," the

Randy and Paula Whites, Joyce Meyers, Benny Hinns, and hundreds of others; can they not make the same claims? There is true faith at work. The blind sheep work and the wolves fleece them.

When it comes to faith and reason, they are incompatible. Anyone who advocates theism—the belief in the supernatural—simultaneously advocates irrationalism—the belief in the unknowable.

The normal response to Christians' acceptance of such values, especially here in the U.S., is predictable. It is their choice. They're hurting no one, and have the freedom of religion. Contrarily, few understand why atheist object so strenuously. I think the answer is best stated by George H. Smith, in his book Atheism: *The Case Against God*:

> The conflict between reason and faith is not primarily a conflict between the propositions of reason and the propositions of faith: it is a more basic conflict between the epistemological requirements of reason and the nature of faith as a claim to nonrational knowledge. I am arguing that faith as such, faith as an alleged method of acquiring knowledge, is totally invalid—and as a consequence, all propositions of faith, because they lack rational demonstration, must conflict with reason.

> The incompatibility of reason and faith does not hinge on whether the nonbeliever can provide knowledge which is in direct contradiction to articles of faith. The full weight of responsibility rests with the Christian: he is offering the articles of faith, and he must demonstrate their compatibility with reason. He must show that, although his propositions lack rational demonstration, they should be accepted as true none-the-less. If he fails to do this, his beliefs collapse as unsupported subjective whims.

RELIGIOUS FAITH

I have no faith and that is accounted evil; but the world if it is saved will be saved by men of goodwill of much thought and of little faith... Faith stops thinking, and thought is the root of life without which we become beasts, faith is surrender and dependence and becoming children again, it is refusing to accept the unimaginable variety of truth and the unwillingness to permit another his variant. Faith stops progress, and legitimizes murder ...

The Frank Yerby quote above, though taken from a work of fiction, *The Saracen Blade*, sums up the fallacy of religions. For, as it states, faith stops thinking, and men who deny their physical senses deny reason. And, if one denies reason there are no guidelines for truth. If one accepts faith as sufficient proof of a god, then we can use that same blind belief in faith to support Santa Claus, leprechauns, and unicorns—or as some believe, even a Satan.

Without thought, we would revert to the superstitious Dark Agess when science was equated with necromancy, and mathematics was declared a tool of the devil. Faith without reason is equivalent to airliners without control towers, or automobiles without steering wheels. In regard to religion, faith is only an excuse to believe the preposterous.

Faith is surrender and dependence. In most cases, especially that of Christianity, truth is defined for the believer who is expected to submit to Church teachings and authority. Such a believer is taught to adhere to set values, generally in the order of God, Church, family, etc. However, what if there is no God? After all, there is no physical proof to support the existence of a god. Gods can only be known intuitively. What if that intuition is nothing more than man's subconsciousness struggling to fulfill perceived values? Then imagine the waste of time, effort, and resources.

According to one census, a third of the world population is Christian, over two billion people throughout the world. Just the ten percent annual tithes generated within those families present a colossal sum—most of which is squandered each year in self-perpetuation. Billions upon billions of dollars expended annually to build more churches, to bring in more converts, and to raise more revenue. Imagine what could be accomplished if those funds were diverted to address such problems as solving the world energy crisis, global warming, or providing medical, educational, and economic aid to underdeveloped countries—or simply to feed, treat, and train the homeless? Imagine a United States where no one lives on the streets. Consider the wasted time. What if everyone dedicated their Sundays to satisfying community needs? Now, imagine if all other religions were induced to follow similar guidelines. Imagine no religious conflicts, no terrorists, or religious warfare. To paraphrase John Lennon—imagine a world without religions.

Faith is becoming children again. Children tend to ignore responsibilities. They would much rather an adult solve all the annoying problems. They'd rather play and enjoy themselves than study and reason. And, should a question arise, it's so much easier to ask an adult rather than seek the answer. The majority of Christians are like children; they're only interested in the "Bible Stories." Many don't even understand the Bible and blindly place their lives, and the lives of their family, in the hands of other human beings. Very few question the validity of the Scriptures, and if they do find contradictions during their studies, they quickly hide any doubt behind the blinders of faith. They are dependent, afraid to trust their own intellect.

They refuse to accept the unimaginable variety of truth. The Bible is a model of misology—the hatred of reason. From the beginning, in the Garden of Eden, the desire for knowledge was stamped as evil. Paul also had much to say against knowledge and wisdom:

> See to it that no one makes a prey of you by philosophy and empty deceit, according to human tradition, according to the elemental spirits of the universe, and not according to Christ" (Col. 2:8).

> For it is written, I will destroy the wisdom of the wise, and will bring to nothing the understanding of the prudent. Where is the wise? Where is the scribe? Where is the disputer of this world? Hath not God made foolish the wisdom of this world? (I Cor. 1:19&20).

Has he? Quite the contrary, the wisdom of this world has made the word of God foolishness. In the early days of the Church, they rejected many truths that cannot be ignored today because those truths have been proven by scientific studies: physics, astronomy, anthropology, archeology, and history. Tertullian, one of the foremost Church fathers, stated, "It is philosophy [ancient sciences] that supplies the heresies with their equipment." And, he wished "a plague on Aristotle."

Martin Luther called reason:

> "... the devil's bride," a "beautiful whore" and "God's worst enemy."..."There is on earth among all dangers," Luther writes, "no more dangerous thing than a richly endowed and adroit reason, especially if she enters into spiritual matters which concern the soul and God. For it is more possible to teach an ass to read than to blind such a reason and lead it right; for reason must be deluded, blinded, and destroyed."..."Faith must trample under foot all reason, sense, and understanding, and whatever it sees it must put out of sight, and wish to know nothing but the word of God."

When Galileo asserted that the sun was the center of our solar system, and tried to defend that position, the Catholic Church avowed the idea "atheistic." The Church, sanctioned by Pope Paul V, decreed Galileo's theory false and contrary to Holy Scripture. Galileo, facing the prospects of prison, was forced to recant. One of his foremost persecutors, the Dominican father Caccini, was said to have declared that "geometry is of the devil," and that "mathematicians should be banished as the authors of all heresies."

St. Augustine, considered by many to be the greatest of the Catholic fathers, opposed reason. His opposition led him to point out that there were many "marvels" in nature that reason could not account for; "wonders of God's working" that "the frail mind of man cannot explain ... ." What were some of those "wonders": the "antiseptic nature" of the peacock that prevented it from rotting; a fountain that lighted quenched torches; and mares in Capadocia that were impregnated by the wind. Reason has freed us from such ignorance and superstitions. Do we really want to cling to the past?

This hatred of reason is one of the Bible's most repulsive traits. The constant demand that one must believe without evidence or thought, that stupidity is a desirable aspect of Christianity is a terrible policy. And what can be a greater lie than the bond between faith and virtue. Doubt and disbelief is equated with immorality; one cannot question the Christian doctrine by reason, instead one must believe blindly or be condemned as immoral.

I'm sure that about now my reader is thinking: "All that was back in the Dark Ages, we're more enlightened now." Yes, you're right—but would we be so without thinkers such as Galileo, Newton, Darwin, Einstein, Dawkins, or Stephen Hawking? Without "men of goodwill of much thought and of little faith" might we not still be in those Dark Ages?

There are many truths in our world and few, such as the ones mentioned above, are absolute. Truth to one might not be recognized as such by another, and what is truth in one instance might not be so in another. We live in a constantly changing world where knowledge is imperfect, for that reason blind, unsubstantiated faith without analytical investigation is a very foolish and dangerous assumption. Can logic or scientific deductions answer every question? Of course not, there are many things science, reason, and logic cannot answer for us; but use of this standard does not lock us into ignorant, irreversible, and sometimes destructive false convictions. We are ignorant of many truths because we refuse to release erroneous ideas. Blind faith in the presumed existent of a god is one of those ideas.

"Faith stops progress, and legitimizes murder ..." Just study the history of Christianity, Islam, Judaism, Hinduism, the old pagan worships—almost any religion—and you'll find the most horrendous, wicked, despotic organizations that ever existed upon this earth. By what law, what reason, can mass religious genocide be condoned? Is there any such thing as a righteous holy war? Can it be the will of a benevolent deity that we exterminate one another in his name? Is there one true form of worship—one correct religion? If so, how do we determine the *chosen* one? Is it enough to rely on faith? Does the self-assurance that swells your breast in righteous indignation not also beat within the Hindu, the Moslem, Jew, or pagan? In the end there is only one difference between you and that heathen and it isn't because you were lucky enough to just stumble upon *the truth*—it's simply your place of birth. Had you been born in China you would, in all probability, be an adherent of Buddhism. In India you would probably be a disciple of Vishnu. In Iraq or Afghanistan, today you might be a walking bomb for Islam. And, don't be so naïve as to think your god ordained your place of birth. People think and derive conclusions in the same manner—only circumstances change the values. And the major disruptive difference is religious faith.

NEW TESTAMENT
CONTRADICTIONS

Many Christians, when confronted with Bible contradictions, excuse such conflicts by assuming it isn't meant that they should understand, that now they "see through a glass darkly" and one day all will be revealed. When others confront them with such questions, they assume the questioner isn't seeing things clearly.

I have met Christians who deny the existence of contradictions in the Bible. When they are presented with obviously contradicting Scriptures they rationalize them with meandering metaphysical or epistemological discourses, or ridiculous explanations that can only be accepted by faith. The reason and origin of such contradictions and interpolations become obvious if one simply considers the history of the Christian religion and its early adherents. In doing so we are confronted with our first contradiction—that of the originator of Christianity.

Christ or the Messiah?

I think I may safely say most Christians believe Jesus was the originator of their religion. To prove their argument they turn to passages that testify of Jesus' miraculous birth, his baptism, and resurrection. They quote such verses as:

Whosoever therefore shall confess me before men, him will I also confess before my Father which is in heaven (Matthew 10:32)

All things are delivered unto me of my Father: and no man knoweth the Son, but the Father; neither knoweth any man the Father, save the Son, and he to whomsoever the Son will reveal him (Matthew 11:27).

He that believeth and is baptized shall be saved; but he that believeth not shall be damned (Mark 16:16).

For God so loved the world, that he gave his only begotten Son, that whosoever believeth in him should not perish, but have everlasting life (John 3:16).

The author of the Gospel According to John really deifies Jesus with such passages as: 4:36, 5:39, 6:54, 6:68, 10:28, 12:25 & 17:2-3. Of course, that was the author's purpose—to deify Jesus as the Son of God.

There are the parables such as that of the good seed and the tares in Luke 8, and that of the wedding in Matthew 22. That these testify to a new salvation through Jesus is deniable because trace roots of Judaism are still evident. In every case, the office of Jesus has been confused. In many cases, the stories are interpolations, or fables, concocted by Hellenistic Jews or gentile converts who had little or no knowledge of the Jewish Law.

Contradictory Scriptures are found in parables that teach observance of the Law—judgment parables such as that of the sheep and goats in which the righteous, the doers of the Law, find grace (Matthew 25), and, as mentioned earlier, in Matt. 5:17-19, which upholds the eternity of the Law. These different teachings are obvious contradictions unless you are willing to admit to two means of salvation—and that is exactly how Christians justify their interpretation. Their explanation is that Jesus first preached salvation to the Jews. Then, when they rejected him, he turned to the Gentiles—and yet, they still claim the Jewish Apostles were ministers to the Gentiles. However, we should acknowledge two distinctions that are often overlooked. First, Jesus was either a Jew or he was not. Being Jewish wasn't just a religion, it was a lifestyle based upon the Hebrew Bible. Therefore, had Jesus fraternized with Gentiles, the unclean, he broke the Law and would have been considered unclean. To purify himself he would have had to undergo a complex purification ritual and we have no record of such an occurrence.

The practice of calling Jesus, *Christ*, is found throughout most of the New Testament. It is important to note that the word *Christ* is Greek for the Hebrew word messiah (mashiyach), or messias (yitshar), meaning anointed or anointing. The Dead Sea Scrolls and early writers such as Josephus, Clement, and Origen make it evident that messianic expectations were widespread in Judea during the first century. In fact, messianic fanaticism was one of the factors that fueled the Jewish War. The Jews were looking for an anointed deliverer, a messiah, and many believed Jesus was that Messiah. And yet, the word messiah is recorded only twice in the New Testament. The reason is because it was translated into the Greek, *Christ*—which is recorded five hundred and sixty-two times. The root can be traced back to the early Christians' use of the Septuagint translation of the Jewish Scriptures. In that translation of the Old Testament the word *messiah* is used thirty-nine times and in every case it is rendered *Christos*—Christ. No wonder the identity of the Jewish messiah was transformed into a Hellenistic god. This makes it almost certain that the changes were adopted from the Septuagint and that the New Testament authors were Hellenistic Jews, rather than Hebraic Jews. Even so, the writers, or translators, of the New Testament have effectively destroyed the identity of a Jewish messiah and replaced it with a Greek god/man by the simple act of distorting the meaning of one word. However, even according to Christian tradition, there can be no doubt Jesus taught that he was the Messiah. As stated in the Gospel of John—the only instances where *messiah* is used. Speaking of the newly converted Andrew:

> He first findeth his own brother Simon, and saith unto him, "We have found the Messias," which is, being interpreted, the Christ (John 1:41).

In John 4:25-26 Jesus claims that messiahship:

> The woman saith unto him, "I know that Messias cometh, which is called Christ: when he is come, he will tell us all things." Jesus saith unto her, "I that speak unto thee am he."

Notice the awkward phrases: "being interpreted, the Christ" and "which is called Christ." If the Gospels were of Hebraic origin then this passage would obviously be a Grecian insertion intended to identify the Messiah as Christ to gentile readers. Such identifying statements would not have been necessary if the readers had been Hebraic Jews. Imagine a Hebraic Jew making such senseless statements as: "We have found the Messias, which is, being interpreted, the Messiah" or "I know that Messias cometh, which is called Messiah." Here is scriptural proof that Jesus was viewed as the Messiah; and, more importantly, the author has Jesus claiming to be that Messiah in John 4:26.

To provide further proof that Jesus was a Jewish messiah rather than the Christian Christ we must introduce another contradiction.

The founder of Christianity—Jesus or Paul?

If Jesus was not the founder of Christianity, who was? The answer is so obvious I'm surprised that it is an issue. Most Christians, theologians, and Bible scholars agree that Paul was the earliest author of New Testament writings. He is credited with authoring thirteen books, but six of those are probably not his works. He is the only New Testament author we can actually name with any degree of assurance. Because of this fact, great emphasis is placed upon the accuracy of his works, and in those works he claims to be the originator of his message:

> But I certify you, brethren, that the gospel which was preached of me is not after man. For I neither received it of man, neither was I taught it, but by the revelation of Jesus Christ (Galatians 1: 11-12).

Paul claimed he received his doctrines from a spiritual Jesus. What were some of those doctrines? Of course, the main teaching had to be salvation through belief in the resurrection of Jesus. Other major points that conflicted with the Jewish teachings were: negation of the sacrifice and circumcision—or the law of the clean and unclean.

These had to be doctrines introduced by Paul, because the Jerusalem Jews—Jesus' disciples—were still teaching obedience to the Law. Some argue that Paul's ministry was to the Gentiles and that the Jews were to the Jews. In fact, such was stated by Paul and the disciples (Romans 15:16, Galatians 2:7&9). Paul even said Jesus' ministry was unto the Jews while his (Paul's) was to the Gentiles:

Now I say that Jesus Christ was a minister of the circumcision for the truth of God, to confirm the promises [made] unto the fathers:

So, was there one mission to the Jews and another to the Gentiles? Must Jews acknowledge Jesus as the Christ to be saved? According to Paul—yes:

[Is] the law then against the promises of God? God forbid: for if there had been a law given which could have given life, verily righteousness should have been by the law. But the scripture hath concluded all under sin, that the promise by faith of Jesus Christ might be given to them that believe (Galatians 3:21&22).

If so, we must assume that all Jesus' disciples were lost because the last information we have of them, at Paul's arrest, they were keeping the Law and trying to get Paul to also.

We must also answer the question: If neither the Jews nor Gentiles were to keep the Law—who was? We quoted Scriptures earlier that assured the eternity of the Law.

The Resurrection

The latest date for the crucifixion of Jesus was probably 36 CE. Mark was the first gospel, written about 66-70 CE, Matthew came next, 85-90 CE, followed a few years later by Luke, and John around 110 CE.

Jesus referred very distinctly to his death and resurrection during his ministry, for example:

When they came together in Galilee, he said to them, "The Son of Man is going to be betrayed into the hands of men. They will kill him, and on the third day he will be raised to life." And the disciples were filled with grief. (Matt. 17:22-23, NIV)

"We are going up to Jerusalem, and the Son of Man will be betrayed to the chief priests and the teachers of the Law. They will condemn him to death and will turn him over to the Gentiles to be mocked and flogged and crucified. On the third day he will be raised to life!" (Matt. 20:18-19, NIV)

He then began to teach them that the Son of Man must suffer
many things and be rejected by the elders, chief priests and
teachers of the Law, and that he must be killed and after three
days rise again. (Mk. 8:31, NIV)

"But after I have risen, I will go ahead of you into Galilee." (Mk.
14:28, NIV)

Yet, after the women found the empty tomb, neither they nor
the disciples could even imagine that Jesus had risen. We read
statements such as:

When they heard that Jesus was alive and that she had seen
him, they did not believe it. (Mk. 16:13, NIV)

These returned and reported it to the rest; but they did not believe
them either. (Mk. 16:13, NIV)

When they saw him, they worshipped him; but some doubted.
(Matt. 28:17, NIV)

They still did not understand from Scripture that Jesus had to rise
from the dead. (Jn. 20:9, NIV)

It is generally supposed that the disciples couldn't understand
because they had not yet received the Holy Spirit. But it should be
obvious that the situation didn't call for spiritual discernment, only
common sense. Even a child of five or six understands statements
such as the ones Jesus allegedly used—a fact which casts doubt on
the validity of those Scriptures. Did Jesus really believe he would die
and rise again? Or was the idea introduced later?

Consider other events: the resurrection of Lazarus along with
the other miracles Jesus supposedly performed. Allegedly, the
disciples saw all this, knew the power of Jesus, and still could not
believe in his death and resurrection.

At his death, according to Matt. 27:52&53, the graves were
opened and the saints arose and went into the holy city and appeared
to many. Do you suppose these resurrected saints told of Jesus'
resurrection? Perhaps they couldn't talk. If so, what form could they
have had? And where did they go afterwards—back to their graves?

Perhaps they were zombies, walking dead indeed, or ghosts without substance. If so, could they really be considered resurrected?

This introduces more interesting facts concerning the reliability of the Gospels. Although the Gospels were written early, late 1st century to early 2nd century, they're never quoted in any of the later New Testament writings. Not even in the Acts of the Apostles, allegedly written by Luke.

Old vs. New Testament Contradictions

The contradictions between the Old and New Testament are so numerous it's impossible to harmonize them. The most common explanation, which we touched on earlier, is that of the *old law* and the *new law*. The Jews were (or are) under the old, impossible to keep, Hebraic Law. Christians observe the spiritual law of Christ. Here, we find another contradiction.

Referring back to Matthew 5:15&16, we find Jesus assuring the eternity of the Law, or commandments—yet repeatedly we find Paul either changing *jots and tittles* or outright negating them.

Therefore by the deeds of the law there shall no flesh be justified in his sight: for by the law [is] the knowledge of sin (Romans 3:20).

Therefore we conclude that a man is justified by faith without the deeds of the law (Romans 3:28).

But that no man is justified by the law in the sight of God, [it is] evident: for, The just shall live by faith (Galatians 3:11).

Wherefore the law was our schoolmaster [to bring us] unto Christ, that we might be justified by faith. But after that faith is come, we are no longer under a schoolmaster (Galatians 3:24&25).

For Christ [is] the end of the law for righteousness to every one that believeth (Romans 10:4).

Having abolished in his flesh the enmity, [even] the law of commandments [contained] in ordinances; for to make in himself of twain one new man, [so] making peace; (Ephesians 2:15).

> But if the ministration of death, written [and] engraven in stones, was glorious, so that the children of Israel could not stedfastly behold the face of Moses for the glory of his countenance; which [glory] was to be done away: (II Corinthians 3:7).

> And they are informed of thee, that thou teachest all the Jews which are among the Gentiles to forsake Moses, saying that they ought not to circumcise [their] children, neither to walk after the customs (Acts 21:21).

And here is a very interesting one:

> For this, Thou shalt not commit adultery, Thou shalt not kill, Thou shalt not steal, Thou shalt not bear false witness, Thou shalt not covet; and if there be any other commandment, it is briefly comprehended in this saying, namely, Thou shalt love thy neighbour as thyself (Rom. 13:9).

Notice that half of the Ten Commandments are lumped under one—a new commandment: *Thou shalt love thy neighbor as thyself.* Even more interesting are the five that are missing: *You shall have no other gods before me. You shall not make for yourself a carved image. You shall not take the name of the Lord your God in vain. Remember the Sabbath day, to keep it holy. Honor your father and your mother.* Do you notice anything these omitted commandments have in common? A few hints: Might Paul be introducing a new god? Could the revered cross be construed as an image? What of the Lord's name? Doesn't proper observance of the Sabbath require adherence to the Law? "For whosoever shall do the will of my Father which is in heaven, the same is my brother, and sister, and mother." All Laws that might conflict with Paul's agenda.

Of course, Paul's teachings were contrary to the Law—what was the Jerusalem Council about? One might argue that Paul was not negating the Law, only offering a freedom from the Law. But the fact that he was condemning circumcision, sacrifice, etc. makes it evident that he was breaking "… one of these least commandments, and teaching men so." Another factor to consider is that by making the Law of no effect, he was destroying it by undermining the foundation of Judaism. Rome, had it chosen, could have devised no better way to destroy the religion and the people.

Few, if any, Christians will deny the validity of the Ten Commandments, the foundation of God's Law. However, they seem to have forgotten that God gave explicit directions as to how they should be observed.

MY GOD

Millions of people choose different gods while others have different concepts of god.

The first Christians were persecuted for their beliefs and openly condemned what they believed to be evil. To stand by and not resist sin was sin itself and they died for their resistance. They sought death because to die was to be with their Lord. (Just like the Muslim extremists of today.) How many Christians today are truly willing to die for their beliefs? How many Christians do you see standing on the street condemning sin: none ... one or two? And are they not thought mad by both Christians and non-Christians? Of course, today Christianity is a socially acceptable religion; it is a must for politicians and fits in comfortably on the five o'clock new. However, the first Christians despised wealth and considered the rich as the enemies of God (See James 2:1-7 & 5:1-4). Isn't America the wealthiest country in the world? The wealth of the early Christians went to feed the poor, the homeless, and widows not into million dollar houses of worship with swimming pools, ball fields, and tennis courts, or TV ministries that bilk fortunes from the needy. The Bible also speaks of those who have a form of Godliness, like many of our politicians, bankers, lawyers, government officials, and businessmen who need to maintain a public appearance. I know I sound harsh, but I am not condemning anyone and I'm not saying how Christians should live. As a matter of fact, I can say that almost all the Christians I have known throughout my life were good, honest, sincere, and loving people. So, you may ask, why am I so opposed to Christianity? I am opposed to anyone accepting a creed or position blindly, on faith, without true knowledge. Be honest with yourself, if you tell someone the Bible is the Word of God shouldn't you prove it so as not to pass on someone else's deception?

My concept of God is really different from what most people believe. Almost all religions envision a supernatural, personalized, all loving, and all caring being; molded from the idea of human imagination. In most cases, as with Christianity and Islam, these gods have given man a book of instructions with rules, or laws, by which they should live. And while those laws may be good, moral codes they have one great flaw—they have been written by or, assuming they were god given, entrusted to man. And man is fallible—therefore the law is fallible. To show what I mean lets look at the Christian Bible.

Let's suppose that the Lord, God, Yahweh (the Jews' name for God) did write the Ten Commandments on tables of stone for Moses, and let's suppose he did dictate the Torah, or Law (the first five books of the Bible) to Moses. Where are the tables? Where is the original manuscript of Moses? Lost? Did they ever exist? We see that even from the beginning we have to believe what someone (we really don't know who) wrote, thousands of years ago. We have to have faith in a fallible, unknown man—actually, many fallible humans.

We are told God chose a people, the Hebrews, to keep and protect his Word, but did they? Did you know that there was at least one time in Hebrew history when their "Law" was lost—a period when the Hebrews did not have the Torah and did not know god? The event can be found in II Kings 22 & II Chronicles 34. The young king Josiah was attacking pagan worship and attempting to lead his people back to Yahweh. While reconstructing the temple the priest, Hilkiah, just happen to "find" the Law of Moses. Here we're back to trusting in man. Did Hilkiah really find the Law, or did he write, or rewrite, it as a way to unite the people under Josiah? At that time no one knew the Law, because we are told that young King Josiah "rent his clothes" upon hearing it read. And how did they know it was really the Law of God? They sent to a prophetess, a soothsayer, for affirmation. So, in this case it wasn't God who was the revelator, but a fallible human—and a witch at that. So, in essence, today the validity of both Judaism and Christianity are not based upon the Bible, the Catholic Church, or God, but the word of a witch.

Another human fallacy of Judaism and Christianity is the fact that their sacred writings, the Bible; is supposed to be the divine revelations of God. However, divine revelations can only occur one on one. That is, I might experience a direct revelation from God, but if I repeat it, it would not be divine. It would only be as valid as my word because of the human element involved. So Moses may have had a divine revelation from God, or Mary, Paul, a Pope, or hundreds of other "saints," but any divine revelation involved could not be passed to the next listener. That means the Bible is subject to human error, and that human error can be seen in the many—thousands—of different scripture readings, and the thousands of differing churches, and thousands of denominations within those churches. You simply cannot have it both ways; there may be either one divine Church, or many humanly conceived churches.

When we look to the Bible for proof of a supreme creator god we find only confusing, contradicting, humanly written passages—that are in most cases utterly ridiculous—and absolutely no proof to back up the stories and teachings claimed. It is at this point that the Christian will turn to faith—belief without evidence. It is here the Christian claims God will reveal himself supernaturally to the believer. And, it is here we must turn again to the question of numerous, conflicting, messages and thousands of differing religions that claim supernatural, personal, revelations. How is it that Christians, Muslims, Zoroastrians, Mystics, Native Americans, Voodoo worshipers, Satanists and thousands of minor, obscure religions—scattered throughout the world—testify to miracles, indwelling spirits, and special knowledge from their god—and yet all differ? How are we to know which—if any—is the true god?

All such confusion vanishes like smoke in a fog bank when we look to the world about us. For what we find is a world build upon the fact that everything that happens has a cause, it is a world based upon knowledge, logic, and scientific facts. The Bible describes an earth created in six days by the spoken command of God. But today, astronomers have disproved that statement simply by observing the gas filled clouds of the nebulas and watching the birth of stars and planets. The Early Church believed the world to be flat; stars and heavenly bodies were living, rational beings, having souls; and the sun and moon were lights suspended in the "firmament" overhead. Those who disputed such teachings were imprisoned, tortured, and often suffered martyrdom at the stake rather than deny what they knew to be true—and these were the intellectuals. Now the knowledge of our solar system is commonly accepted facts taught in our schools. We've even sent cameras to distance planets that send photographs back. We know the stars are burning suns within galaxies of their own.

The Dark Age, a vague 1000 year period of ignorance, superstition, enslavement, torture, genocide, and depravity was introduced and executed by Roman Catholicism. Only the clergy—members of the Church—could read, and only they were allowed to interpret the Bible. All the wonderful knowledge and enlightenment of the early Greek and Roman philosophers and scientists was replaced by the religious superstition of the Church—ignorance reigned. Those who disagreed were declared outlaws and given a year to denounce their beliefs and surrender to the Church's teachings. During that year, as outlaws, the community shunned them. They could not practice their trade. They were not allowed to work, were unable to buy and sale, and there was no recourse to the law. Anyone discovered helping them was subject to the same excommunication. After the year, if they did not repent, they were excommunicated and declared heretics and, as such, were subject to death.

In this way the intellectuals, the thinkers, the brilliant, the leaders of society were either destroyed or corrupted. Millions were slaughtered leaving only the beaten, uneducated, and ignorant. Destroy the best of a society and you destroy the society. The result was a collapse of the economy, with armed bands raiding in the name of the Church, and finally starvation and plagues depopulated the lands. This is the history of Christianity and the legacy of superstition and ignorance. It is the result when men stop thinking. All this is undisputed truth, not even the Catholic Church will deny. In fact they admit it. They admit it because they sincerely believed it was their duty to convert everyone to Christianity or destroy those who refused.

The jealousy with which the Church guards and defends her deposit of faith is therefore identical with the instinctive duty of self-preservation and the desire to live. This instinct is by no means peculiar to the Catholic Church; being natural it is universal. All sects, denominations, confessions, schools of thought, and

associations of any kind have a more or less comprehensive set
of tenets on the acceptance of which membership depends. In
the Catholic Church this natural law has received the sanction of
Divine promulgation, as appears from the teaching of Christ and
the Apostles... https://www.ecatholic2000.com/cathopedia/vol7/
volseven300.shtml

In other words, the Church's animalistic instincts to survive are
sanctioned by God.

I don't, I can't, accept such reasoning. Instead, when I look about
our world I see a wonderfully balanced system of natural laws that
operate without fail. The movement of our planet about the sun
dictates the seasons; the seasons give periods of production and
rest for the earth, which in turn provides life for all living creatures.
The heat of the sun produces the water evaporation—rain cycles to
water the earth. It gives warmth to ferment the seeds and energy for
growing plants. Each year is a dying and rejuvenation for the earth.
And like the earth, all living creatures are born, live, and die in cycles.
These are immutable laws, sure, proven, and unchangeable. There are
physical and mathematical laws; laws that protect the environment
and laws that provide for our health and well-being. They are all
about us. They direct our ways, they regulate our lives, they bless us
when we act within their bounds and they irrevocably, impersonally,
and mercilessly lash us when we transgress. Like it or not, this is our
God, more powerful than all the gods of Olympia, more vengeful
than Yahweh, more of a blessing than Jesus: fair, impartial, and as
enduring as this world of ours.

There are those who believe God, as the creator, is the author of
these laws but they can show no proof. On the other hand, if God did
set them in motion why did the Church deny and suppress them for
so long—as mentioned above?

Am I a Deist, that is, do I believe that the creator god lives in and
is witnessed by nature? No. Unlike many people, I do not believe that
all creation had to come from infinite wisdom. If such an infinite
wisdom did exist, I see no reason why that would automatically
make *it* a God. Quite the contrary; the fact that we have natural
catastrophes—tragedies such as earthquakes, storms, floods and
fires—belie an all wise, all-powerful, benevolent God. However,
the acknowledgment of natural laws explains the seemly unfair

occurrences in life, the death of innocent children, the suffering of the just, and the impersonal selection of diseases. For an omnipotent, omniscient, all loving god to blame the evils of **his** creation upon the original parents, also **his** creation, is only a cop out. Such reasoning is on the same plane as a drunken, destitute father who, unable to buy a gift, tells his child that Santa Claus won't bring her a doll because she's been bad. The excuse protects the inept father and places the guilt upon the innocent child.

The recorded history of man upon earth can be traced back millions, not thousands, of years. Throughout that time men have attempted to create a deity to protect and save them. Religions have risen and disappeared, gods have come and gone, but not one of our natural laws has failed. Catholicism may annihilate heretics, Protestants may promise heaven and threaten hell, Palestinians may bomb Israelis, and Muslims may pray for their Holy War; but no matter their efforts, they will not change **one** natural law—not even if they destroy all humanity. For, assuming our planet remains, the laws will continue to function and eventually life will return to our earth.

Tell me the name of the god who can defy gravity and cause Newton's apple to fly rather than fall to earth. Which god has the power to lengthen the day or shorten the night? Where is the god who can shift the tides of the oceans? Or perhaps these feats are too hard for your god. Perhaps he can do something simple like make one and one equal three? (The contention over the Trinity proves the fallacy of such an endeavor.) No, don't refer me to chapter and verse in your sacred word, fables are not proof, have your god declare the feat, and then perform it in the open. Can you not see that all the gods throughout history are helpless before the laws that govern our world?

What is my religious philosophy then? It is simple; the laws that regulate this world in which we live regulate our lives as well. The same law that tells birds when to migrate or animals to hibernate has given man the ability to collect information through the five senses of sight, taste, touch, smell, and hearing. To collect and analysis this information we have been given a fantastic and amazing brain with which to think and reason. Religions enslave their members and destroy their ability to reason. This is a violation of nature's laws and the results can be found inscribed repeatedly throughout history. Neither being a Christian, Muslim, Hindu, Baptist, atheist, agnostic, nor the promise of eternal life, is of any importance when compared to the surrender of reason.

Despite what religion would have you believe, faith is not a good thing and should not be equated with trust. You trust someone or something of which you have knowledge. Faith demands total, blind, obedience to that which you do not know. It demands a denial of reason. And in the case of religions it is submitting your life, not to a god, but to an organization of men that have been deceived even as they would deceive you.

If you would draw closer to God look to the sciences that govern our world. Look at the blessings and knowledge they have given us in the fields of medicine, mathematics, biology, archeology, technology—think of the wonders yet to be discovered! We have learned much about the laws regulating our world, but there is so much still hidden. Imagine the world without religions; a world where all men realize that it is *Mother Nature* they should fear instead of humanly conceived deities. (And no, I'm not advocating a form of nature worship.) Imagine a world where all men strive to understand the laws that regulate their world and work together for the good of all. Sure it's a far-fetched idea, but one that is a lot more likely than a pie-in-the-sky afterlife, and unlike religions it can be proven and is demonstrated daily in every person's life. Such a philosophy will not always lead you to the *right* decisions, but neither will you be left to helpless prayers and hopeless indecision. The superstitious man sees unusual events as mysterious wonders. The reasonable man sees events as logical occurrences. Knowledge is power because it dispels superstitions and fear.

SUMMATION

If we accept the Christian tale of a savior Son of God all the inconsistencies must be ignored or slicked underneath a heavy slathering of religious mysticism.

Contrarily, I submit that what I have presented is the story of a corruption of a Hebraic messianic expectation. It is a logical story, supported by historical records, New Testament statements, and common sense.

SELECTED BIBLIOGRAPHY

Davidson, Samuel - *The Canon of the Bible*. New York: Peter Eckler Pub. Co., [1917?]

Dungan, David L.—*Constantine's Bible*. Minneapolis: Fortress Press, 2007

Durant, Will—*The Age of Faith*. New York: Simon and Schuster, 1950

Eisenman, Robert—*Dead Sea Scrolls Uncovered*. New York: Penguin Books, 1992

Enslin, Morton Scott—*Christian Beginnings (Part I & II)*. New York: London, Harper & Bros., 1938

Finlan, Stephen—*The Apostle Paul and the Pauline Tradition*. Collegeville: Liturgical Press, 2008

Johnson, Paul—*A History of Christianity*. New York: Atheneum, 1980

Kimball, Charles—*When Religion Becomes Evil*. San Francisco: Harper San Francisco, 2002

Lecky, W.E.H.—*History of the Rise & Influence of the Spirit of Rationalism in Europe*. New York: D. Appleton, 1866

Mack, Burton L.—*Who Wrote the New Testament?* San Francisco: HarperCollins, 1996

Metzger, Bruce M.—*The Text of the New Testament—Its Transmission, Corruption & Restoration*. New York: Oxford University Press, 1992

Moffatt, James—*Introduction to the Literature of the New Testament*. New York: C. Scribner's Sons, 1911

Mosheim, Johann Lorenz von—*Ecclesiastical History*, London: Longman, Orme & Co., 1841

Patzia, Arthur G.—*The Making of the New Testament*. Downers Grove: Inter Varsity Press, 1995

Rosen, William—*Justinian's Flea*. New York: Penguin Group, 2007

Schonfield, Dr. Hugh J.—*The Passover Plot*. New York: Bantam, 1965

Shaff, Philip—*History of the Christian Church*. New York

Soards, Marion L.—*The Apostle Paul: An Introduction to His Writings and Teachings*. New York: Paulist Press, 1987

Von Daniken, Erich—*Miracles of the Gods*. New York: Dell, 1975

Ware, Bishop Kallistos—*The Orthodox Church*. London: Penguin, 1993

Wilson, A. N.—*Paul: The Mind of the Apostle*. New York: W. W. Norton & Company, 1997

Wise, Michael; Abegg Jr., Martin; Cook, Edward—*Dead Sea Scrolls-A New Translation*. San Franciso: Harper San Francisco, 1996

EARLY WRITINGS

Athenagoras of Athens—*A Plea for the Christians*
Epiphanius, Panarion(*Medicine-chest* or *AdversusHaereses, Against Heresies*)
Eusebius, Bishop of Caesarea—*Praeparatio Evangelica*
Felix, Minucius, *Octavius*
Hegesippus—*Hypomnemata*
Hippolytus of Rome (c. 170-c. 236)—*The Refutation of All Heresies*
Irenaeus, Bishop of Lyons—*Adversus Haereres*
Justin Martyr—*First Apology to the Emperor Antoninus Pius*
Papias, Bishop of Hieropolis—*Expositions of the Sayings of the Lord*
(quoted by Eusebius)
Tacitus—*The Annals, Book XV*
Tatian—*Apology to the Greeks*
Tertullian—*Apology; De Spectaculis; De Corona*
Theophilus, Bishop of Antioch—*Autolycus*

INTERNET REFERENCES

Carrier, Richard—*The Formation of the New Testament (2000)*(www.infidels.org/library/modern/richard_carrier/NTcanon.html)
Doherty, Earl—*The Jesus Puzzle.* (http://www.jesuspuzzle.com/)
New Advent Catholic Encyclopedia (http://www.newadvent.org/)
Original Catholic Encyclopedia (http://oce.catholic.com/ indexhp?title=Home)
Ancient History Encyclopedia (www.ancient.eu/hadrian)
The One God in the Trinity Stanford Encyclopedia of Philosophy; section 3.1.1
Dr. James Tabor—*The Jewish Roman World of Jesus* (https://pages.uncc.edu/james-tabor/ancient-judaism/nazarenes-and-ebionites/#:~:text=Nazarenes%20and%20Ebionites%20Josephus%20reports%20four%20main%20sects,Palestinian%20Jewish%20groups%20in%20late%202nd%20Temple%20times.)

ABOUT THE AUTHOR

Photo by Jordyn Ledford

D oyle Duke spent eight years in the U.S. Navy as a photographer's mate. There, he attended three photographic schools, was a designated motion picture photographer, and rose to the rank of First Class before deciding not to make the Navy a lifetime career.

During his career in the real world, his two major employers were the *Chattanooga Times Newspaper* and *Hinkle's Commercial Photographics*. He attended local colleges, studying business and art, and completed one year.

As a young man, he came to love the outdoors, hunting, hiking, biking, and scenic photography. In later years his interests turned to social issues such as over population, pollution, the depletion of our natural resources, racism, and of course, the old, good versus evil puzzle, religion. He has self-published a number of articles and books on these subjects, among them: *The Amazing Deception: A Critical Analysis of Christianity, Extended Vacation,* and two in a future apocalyptic series, *In Search of Camelot* and *Tomorrow's Dreamers.*

He has been married to his lifetime love, Fay Royster Duke, for over fifty-five years. They have two children, four grandchildren, and three great-granddaughters. They live on Brindlee Mountain, just south of Huntsville, Alabama.